Scout Boating

Written by
Terry Stringer and David Sturdee

Edited by
Jim Davidson and Stephen Nixey

Illustrated by
Dave Green

Copyright © 1993
The Scout Association
Baden-Powell House, Queen's Gate, London SW7 5JS
ISBN 0 85165 275 1
First Edition

Contents

Introduction 3

The Junior Seaman Badge 4
Swimming 4
Safety Rules 4
Wind 5
Tides 5
Currents 6
Lifejackets and buoyancy aids 7
Rowing 7
Sculling 9
Sailing 9
Canoeing 10
Knots, bends, hitches and
rope sealing 11

The Seaman Badge 14
Rescue 14
Line throwing 15
Rules and signals for safe boating .. 16
Rules of the road 16
Expeditions afloat 17

The Leading Seaman Badge 19
Pilotage 19
Care and maintenance 20
Weather 20
Weather signs 21
Activities afloat 21

The Master Seaman Badge 23
Signals 23
Charts 24
The compass rose 25
Activity rules 25
Expedition 26

Training Activities 27
Practical skills 27
Pulling 28
Steering 29
Cox a crew 30
Power 32
Canoeing 33
Sailing 34
Anchoring 39
Safety 40
Rescue exercise 42
Man overboard 42
Capsize drill 44

Boats and construction 45
Boats and their care 45
Boat repairs 45
Rigging a sailing boat 50
Jury rig 51
Bosun's bag 51

Navigation 52
Variation, deviation and
compass error 52
More about tides 54
Definitions 55
Plotting a position 58

Ropework and tradition 62
Bosun's call 63
Ropework 64

Meteorology 69

Rule of the road and
communications 75

Safety 75
Danger signals 77
The buoyage system 78
Sound signals 79
Navigation lights 80
Racing rules 82

Expeditions 84

Seamanship

Seamanship has four progressive Proficiency badge stages, the first two of which come in the 'Interest' category, and the second two in the 'Pursuit' category. Sea Scouts will almost certainly want to work through these badges, but they are available for all Scouts to gain. Each of the badges is of the same basic design, but with a different colour for each of the stages.

Introduction

Consistency in the approach to these badges and the understanding of some general standard is obviously important. But also we have to recognise that the natural facilities, leaders' expertise and opportunities vary enormously. Thus this programme includes a great deal of choice: there are easy options, inevitably, but on balance the guidance of adult leadership should be able to produce a meaningful and relevant programme of training, which can be applied in the situation of all groups with any commitment to training in water activities.

Some approach badge work as a series of lessons and tests. This is not really the intention for the operation of the scheme as a whole, but clearly those participating in the scheme need some measure of progress. Much of the training should be done by practical instruction and the operation of an environment within which there is a sound framework of the good practice of a seaman. Assessment should be seen in the light of the regular practical application of what the badges require. There are sufficient items also to support indoor winter training, much with a bias towards the practical.

Work for the badges counts, of course, as part of the Proficiency badge requirements but some also count as part of 'the Scout Award, Pathfinder Award, Explorer Award and the Chief Scout's Award'. Likewise, there is much overlap between some of the optional items and some of the compulsory parts. Specific skills learnt can unquestionably count for as many items as you can find; this is the intention.

The Junior Seaman Badge

Interest

SWIMMING

1. Swim 50 metres and stay afloat for five minutes.

Swimming is a good sport, but for anyone who is keen on water activities, swimming also means safety. Since you have to be able to swim before you can begin your work on the Seamanship badges, you should only need practice to meet this requirement.

Swimming with your boating clothes on is much more tiring than swimming in swimming costumes. Practise also swimming in a lifejacket or buoyancy aid.

You might like to take the Amateur Swimming Awards for proficiency in personal survival.

SAFETY RULES

2. Explain the safety rules that apply to boating and the effects of winds, tides and current.

(i) Wear the right clothing. If it is cold (or might become so) this will include a waterproof top and jersey, possibly even a woolly hat and gloves. In more open or advanced waters you need a wet suit if it is cold. Soft shoes or proper sailing boots; no heavy footwear.

(ii) Use the right personal safety gear: lifejacket or buoyancy aid. For almost all activities in fast running water or playing water polo you will need a proper canoeing crash helmet.

(iii) If you get into difficulties stay with the boat. Swimming is far more likely to lead to disaster because distances are deceptive, you may not realise the strength of the currents and the water may be cold. Also, rescuers cannot see you easily.

(iv) Exercise the good practice of seamanship. That means sensible conduct, remembering all the skills of seamanship you have learnt, and remembering that a small mishap can lead to disaster on the water.

(v) The boat, its buoyancy and equipment must be sound. Report any damage.

(vi) Always canoe in groups of at least three.

(vii) Do not go off without telling someone responsible what you are up to and when you will be back.

(viii) Remember that your skills are limited. Do not go into water which might be more dangerous than you are used to or on a craft which you do not understand unless someone more experienced authorises it.

(ix) Do not assume that other boat users know what they are doing! Be considerate too.

(x) There are Scout Association rules to follow. Your Leader will guide you as appropriate.

WIND

Wind is the movement of air. It is never constant.

Around the coast, winds often blow on to the shore during the day (sea breezes) and offshore at night (land breezes).

This is the normal local pattern and it will not apply if stronger winds are affecting the area.

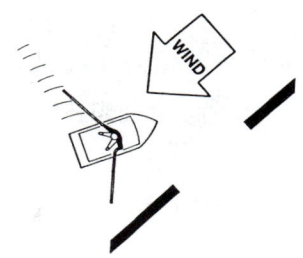

Strong winds mean high waves. Keep your boat heading into strong winds and waves. They will tend to turn the boat broadside on, causing it to roll, and in rough weather waves will break over the side of the boat. You have to counteract this by heading into the wind.

TIDES

Tide is the movement of the water caused by the varying positions of the earth, moon and sun. When these are all in line, at full or new moon, spring tides occur. The tide comes in, or floods, and goes out, or ebbs, further at these times than during neap-tides, which occur when the moon is at right angles to the line of the earth and sun. The tide usually floods for about 6¼ hours and ebbs for about 6¼ hours.

Remember

It is hard to pull or row against the wind.

The wind can blow you off course, so head to windward, i.e. the direction from which the wind is blowing.

Spring and neap-tides occur alternately for periods of about 7½ days (a quarter of a lunar month).

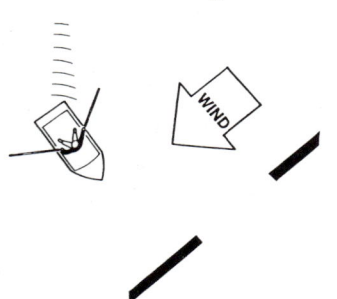

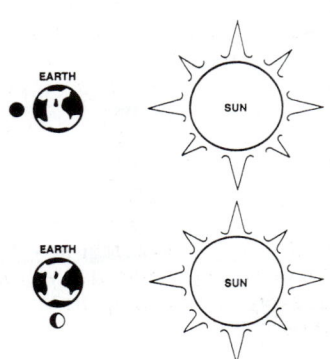

The Junior Seaman Badge

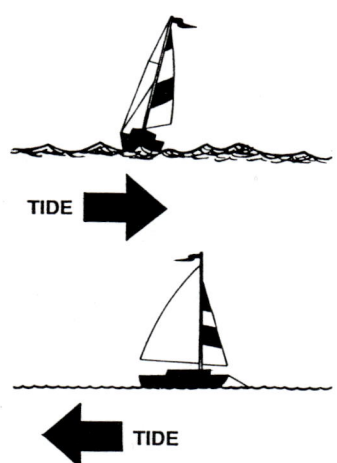

TIDE →

TIDE ←

When the wind is blowing against the tide (weather going tide) the water will be rough. When it blows in the same direction as the tide (lee going tide) conditions will be calmer.

Tides run more strongly in midstream and on the outside of curves in rivers, and off headlands at sea.

Remember

Going against the tide may be difficult and it may be impossible. Plan to go with the tide at all times. If this is not practical, try to go out against the tide so that you can come back with it. You will be more tired at the end of your journey and you do not want to leave the worst part till last.

The rise and fall of the tide will affect anchorage. Leave enough slack to allow for this.

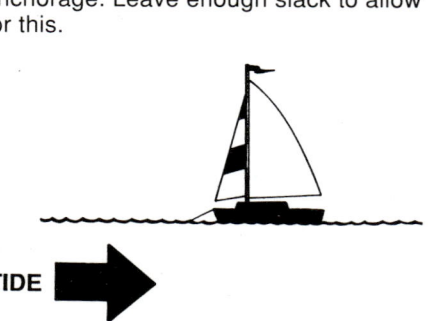

TIDE →

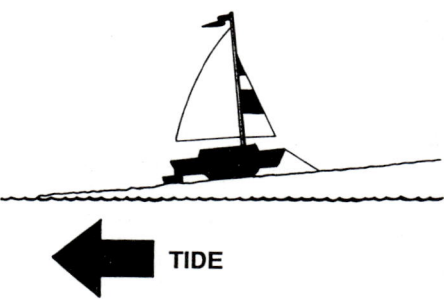

TIDE ←

CURRENTS

Current is the movement of water caused by the wind and gravity.

Set off or come alongside heading into the current, or upstream. Only then can you keep complete control of your boat. Even though you seem to be stationary, you will maintain steerage way, since you are really moving against the current.

Strong onshore winds may cause a great accumulation of water near the beach. This creates an undertow which can be very dangerous when swimming and when disembarking from boats.

LIFEJACKETS AND BUOYANCY AIDS

3. **Explain the difference between a buoyancy aid and a lifejacket. Adjust to fit and wear one to enter the water from a height of one metre.**

You must be very familiar with the whole subject of lifejackets - when and how to put them on, their maintenance and proper care. Lifejackets must be either to a pattern approved by the British Standards Institute to BS.3595 (1981) and Kitemarked or to the European Standard and marked with the EC symbol. Ideally the British Standard type should have at least 6.2 kg of inherent buoyancy, inflatable to a total of 16 kg buoyancy. The European Standard should have a minimum of 150 Newtons of buoyancy. Buoyancy aids should be to a pattern approved by the British Marine Industry Federation (BMIF), the British Canoe Union, British Canoe Manufacturers' Association (BCU/BCMA BA33) or the European Standard (EC) and marked with their symbol of approval. Lifejackets are so designed that they should turn an unconscious person face up in less than 5 seconds and keep that person in a position so that they can breathe.

Lifejackets must be worn when sailing or canoeing in tidal waters. When rowing, they must be carried ready to be put on in the event of low visibility, rough weather or broken water.

In a canoe, never inflate a lifejacket until you are well clear of the cockpit. An inflated lifejacket could prevent you getting out!

Put your lifejacket on securely. However efficient it is, it will be no good to you if it comes off.

PRACTICAL

4. **Complete ONE of the following:**

ROWING

(a) **Row a dinghy single-handed and carry out basic manoeuvres.**

Good rowing comes after a lot of practice. Set yourself a high standard.

Sit in the middle of the thwart, facing the stern.

Adjust the stretcher so that your legs are straight. This gives you the best possible drive as you make your stroke.

Place the crutches in the sockets. One arm of the crutch may be longer than the other. Place the crutch so that the longer arm is nearer the bow.

Place the oar with the leathered part in the crutch.

Lean forward with your back and your arms straight.

Raise your arms and put the blades of the oars into the water.

The Junior Seaman Badge

Lean backwards and drive your legs and feet hard against the stretcher. Pull with your arms, bending them only when your body is passing through the vertical position. Keep your elbows into your sides and draw the oars into your chest. This should be a horizontal movement with the oars maintaining a constant depth in the water and the handles remaining at the same height above the gunwale.

As the oar handles reach your chest, drop your hands to bring the oars out of the water.

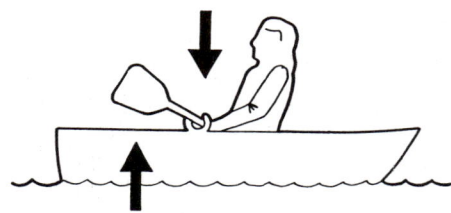

Swing forward keeping your back and arms straight and repeat the movement, keeping the oars immersed as you pull and clear of the water as you lean forward each time.

To maintain a straight course, line up with two aligned objects on the shore and keep them in line. Check frequently to see that there are no objects, swimmers or other craft in your way. To do this, glance over your shoulder as you lean forward to start a new stroke.

Both oars should enter and leave the water together and they should be pulled at the same rate. Do not watch your oars.(You cannot watch both at once, and you would be inclined to pull harder on the oar that you are watching. This could take you off course.)

There are two ways of altering course.

1. Pull on one oar harder than the other, or on one oar only while holding the other out of the water.

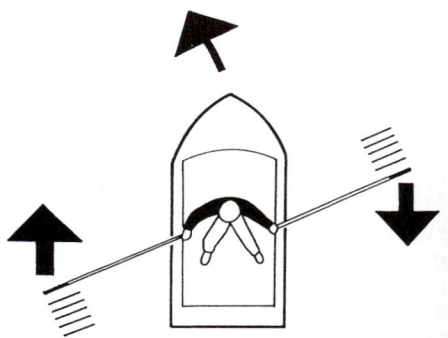

2. Pull on one oar whilst pushing with the other.

To stop the boat in an emergency, drop both blades into the water and hold the oars still. This is called holding water. It is, of course, more difficult the faster the boat is moving.

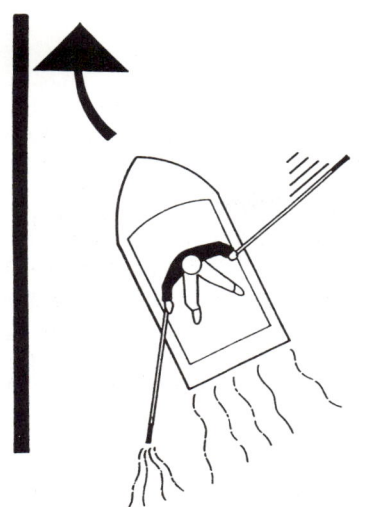

When you come alongside it is often possible to hold water on just one side so the boat turns and stops. Mind your oars as you come in. Always stow oars and crutches before you get out, and moor the boat properly.

SCULLING

(b) Scull a dinghy over the stern and carry out basic manoeuvres.

When you first try sculling over the stern, you will not find it particularly easy; so you want to start in very calm conditions if possible.

It is a method of propelling a boat used by one person with only one oar.

Stand feet apart and legs braced.

Place the oar in the sculling notch or crutch and hold the grip with both hands, thumbs underneath.

The oar is then moved through a figure of eight stroke, so that the water is pressing on the same side of the oar all the time.

As your sculling improves, you will be able to work the oar with only one hand, while standing sideways to watch where you are going.

If the blade is held slightly flatter as you move it in one direction than the other the boat will turn. Major turns can be made more crudely by repeated strokes in one direction only.

Once you have mastered going in a straight line you should practise sculling round buoys, picking up objects in the water, and coming alongside.

SAILING

(c) Sail a figure of eight course.

Here you are expected to show that you have made a successful start at sailing. Someone may help you launch and rig the boat, and get away from the shore if circumstances make it difficult.

Note that you cannot sail directly into the wind; the diagram shows a no go zone.

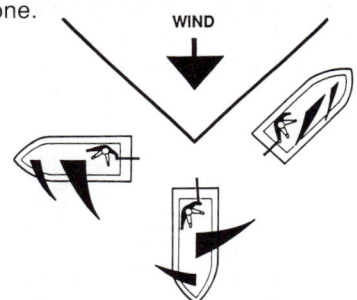

The next two diagrams show the different courses which you are expected to steer.

The Junior Seaman Badge

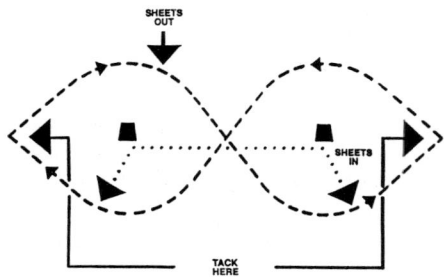

The first involves tacking, where the boat is turned into the wind. Remember that you cannot sail in the no go zone, and hence the sharp bend in the course. Keep the tiller over while you go

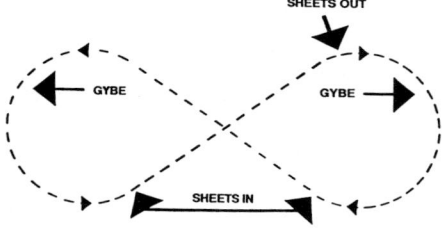

about, and let the sheets out as you turn away from the wind. Pull them in again as you turn your back into the wind.

The second involves gybing, where you turn away from the wind. Adjust the sheets as before. As you gyb, hand the boom over in good time, and straighten the tiller as the boom comes over.

It is not essential to use buoys for this exercise, but they will help you provided that they are not too close.

CANOEING

(d) Qualify for the BCU One Star test.

This test is designed as a basic assessment of ability. You are most likely to take this test after a short course, either over a weekend or a number of evenings. If you are not new to the activity, and have a certain amount of experience, then it is always possible for a direct assessment to be made. The test falls into three parts, a theory part and two practical parts.

The theory part covers a basic knowledge of canoeing equipment

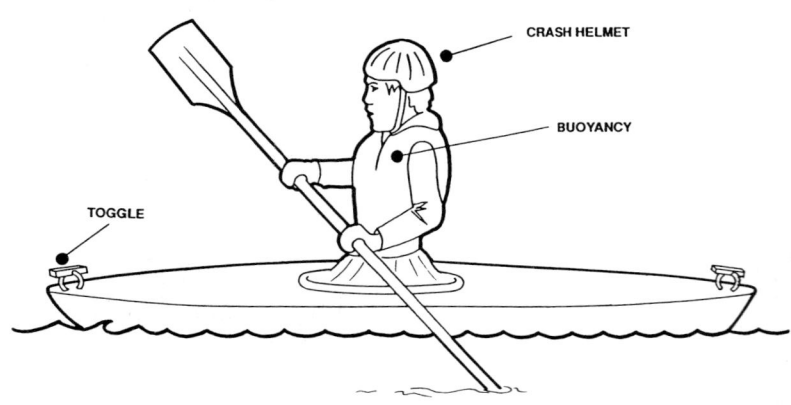

(personal dress, lifejackets, spraydeck and paddle) as well as the canoe itself. Furthermore, knowledge of capsize drill and action to be taken is required.

The first practical part requires you to perform certain skills satisfactorily. These cover launching the canoe, getting into it, paddling and then returning to the bank and disembarking. Whilst afloat you will have to demonstrate paddling both forwards and backwards, turning the canoe, stopping in both directions, and forward and reverse sweeps. In addition you will have to demonstrate a capsize and swim ashore.

The second practical part only requires you to show, satisfactorily, beginnings in the execution of certain basic canoeing strokes, i.e. the Support and Draw strokes and stern rudders.

If you are starting out as a novice (or maybe even an 'old hand') in this activity a very good book for you to read is *CANOEING - Skills and Techniques* by Neil Shave, details of which are contained in a bibliography at the end of this publication.

RYA

(e) Gain the RYA National Dinghy Certificate Scheme Level 1.

The aim of this course is to provide a brief taste of dinghy sailing for novices. By the end of the course participants will have had a short introduction to the sport of dinghy sailing, including basic boat handling techniques and essential background knowledge.

The instruction and assessment are practical and theoretical. You will be able to launch and recover your dinghy, carry out simple sailing techniques such as tacking, gybing and stopping. In addition you will be introduced to safety considerations.

KNOTS, BENDS, HITCHES AND ROPE SEALING

5. Carry out an activity using a knot, a bend, a hitch and a lashing, and demonstrate rope sealing.

Many knots are described, with illustrations, in a number of The Scout Association's publications, the most comprehensive of which are *Scout Pioneering* by John Sweet and *The SCOUTING Magazine Book of Knots* by Eric Franklin. You should be able to tie all these knots without hesitation. A good way of finding out if you really know how to tie a knot is to see if you can do it with your eyes shut.

The REEF KNOT is used in sailing to tie in the battens in the sails where necessary and to tie surplus sail above the boom when it is reefed during high winds. It is not very strong when tied in ropes of synthetic fibres.

The FISHERMAN'S BEND is sometimes called the Anchor bend, and this tells you what it is used for - to attach an anchor to a rope or warp. It is similar to the round turn and two half hitches, but more suitable to a jerking pull. It is inclined to jam and cannot be cast off easily.

The SHEET BEND is used to bend a line to an eye splice or for bending two lines together.

The BOWLINE gives a non-slip loop and is very important in life-saving. You should be able to tie it around yourself and around a person facing you. It is also used in place of the loop when tying a Sheet Bend if the rope is to be under tension. It is also ideal for mooring small craft, but remember that it cannot be undone under tension.

The DOUBLE SHEET BEND is also used to bend together two ropes of unequal thickness.

It is particularly suitable for use with synthetic and wet ropes.

The SAILMAKER'S WHIPPING. Whippings are used to stop the ends of ropes and to repair a frayed end. The Sailmaker's is very secure and will not slip off.

Most ropes used now are synthetic. When you cut these, make a point of sealing the ends. This is best done with a proper electric cutting gun, but you are unlikely to have access to one. A gas flame, candle flame or simply a lighted match will do the trick. Try not to melt too much of the rope, it will go hard if you do. Squash the end of the rope back into shape whilst it is soft, by working in on a suitable surface. Your fingers will not stand the heat!

The ROUND TURN AND TWO HALF HITCHES is used for making fast a boat's painter to a ring or post. It will never jam and can be cast off quickly, even under tension.

If you are going to splice or whip the rope then seal each strand separately. Where possible, whippings and splices are still advisable if you want the end to last.

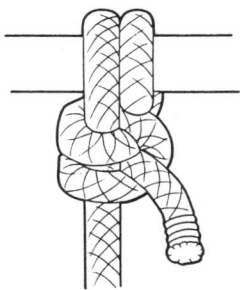

You are likely to use some form of lashing to secure a boat or canoe on a trailer or roof-rack. Alternatively, you may lash equipment in a boat so it is secure while sailing or being towed.

TRAINING ACTIVITIES

6. **From the list of training activities, complete six items from at least four of the sections.**

You must choose to suit your interests, the expertise around to instruct you, and the facilities you have. Advice on this part is given further on in this publication as these items apply to other stages of these badges as well.

GET THESE BADGES!

Here are three badges that you might think of working for as you move on to the next stage of your training.

Elementary Helmsman
(Interest)

Swimmer
(Interest)

Elementary Canoeist
(Interest)

The Junior Seaman Badge

The Seaman Badge

Interest

1. Hold the Junior Seaman badge, or be at least 11½ years of age, and complete requirements 1, 2, 3 and 5 of the Junior Seaman badge.

These are very basic skills necessary for safety of people and equipment, so they must not be omitted!

RESCUE

2. Have some knowledge of rescue by boat or canoe and be able to carry out a simple rescue exercise.

If the person in the water is not wearing a lifejacket or buoyancy aid, throw out something that will float for the person to hold on to. Be careful not to hit them!

If you are strong enough, and in a small boat, get the person in over the stern, while the crew steadies the boat. Take care that the boat does not turn over onto the casualty.

If you are not strong enough to do this, but are within reasonable distance of the shore or bank tow the person to the shore. This technique can be used in a canoe too.

Watch the person or, if you are busy with another part of the rescue, tell someone else to watch the person.

If sailing, approach on a close reach so that you have maximum control over the boat and its speed.

Remember

Speed is essential. The person may be injured or suffering from shock. The longer the casualty stays in the water, the greater the danger of hypothermia (loss of core body heat).

LINE THROWING

3. Heave a lifeline from a boat, to land within reach of a target six metres away, within two attempts.

First practise throwing a line on shore to improve your accuracy.

Line throwing is important and useful. When you need to throw a line, you need to be quick and accurate. Whether mooring or rescuing a person in the water, success first time is always best. *Scout Pioneering* will tell you how to go about it and how to prepare the line so that it goes out properly.

Remember

Coil the rope properly, even if this takes a little time. If you are throwing from a sailing dinghy or canoe, you will have to throw from a sitting position. This is much more awkward and calls for a lot of practice.

You should also be able to throw a lifebuoy effectively. You will have to throw underarm and, again, aim at a point near the casualty so that they can swim to it. Haul in slowly and steadily. Quick jerky pulls will drag the casualty under.

RULES AND SIGNALS FOR SAFE BOATING

4. Know the steering and sailing rules and apply these to the craft being used.

Steering and sailing rules apply when vessels are on a collision course. This means that unless one or the other takes action, a collision will be inevitable. Like all rules, these rules do our thinking for us, and save us from having to work out the best course of action. If we follow them, there will be no danger and no delay.

To find out if another vessel is on a collision course with your own, take a bearing on it. If this bearing remains constant, then you are both on a collision course. It is not necessary to take the bearing with a compass. You may just line up the vessel with a part of your own boat and see if it stays in the same position. Of course, your vessel should not alter course while you are checking.

These rules apply to all craft.

1. In general, power craft give way to sailing vessels.
2. Overtaking vessels must keep clear of the vessel being overtaken until the possibility of collision is past. A vessel is overtaking if it is approaching from more than 2 points (i.e. 22½ degrees) abaft the beam of the other.
3. Small craft must not impede larger craft which cannot alter course quickly or are restricted to deep water channels.
4. Remember that when you are in a canoe or rowing craft, your boat is more manoeuvrable than most power craft, and you should, therefore, give way to them. Otherwise, canoes and rowing craft are considered as power craft.
5. Regardless of rules, when action taken by the appropriate vessel will not of itself avert collision, it is the responsibility of other craft to take whatever action is necessary.
6. Different rules apply to vessels when racing. It is customary to keep clear of racing vessels.
7. Keep a good lookout at all times.

RULES OF THE ROAD

Sailing vessels

When two sailing vessels have the wind on a different side, the one with the wind on her port side gives way.

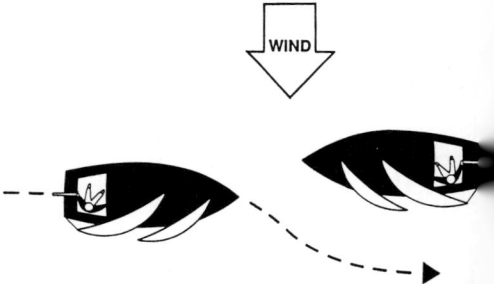

When the vessels have the wind on the same side, the one to windward gives way.

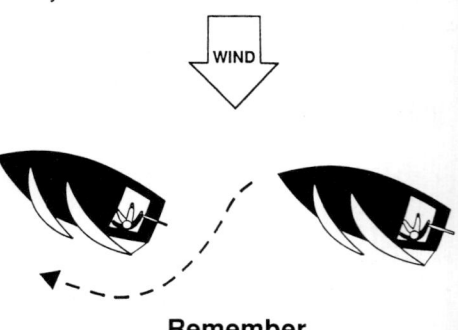

Remember

Overtaking vessels always keep clear.

Power driven vessels

When two power driven vessels are meeting head on or nearly head on, each must alter course to starboard.

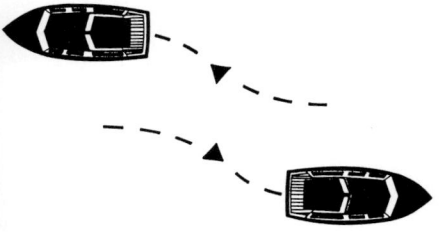

When two power driven vessels are on converging courses, the one with the other to starboard gives way.

A power driven vessel gives way to a sailing vessel except in a narrow channel where a power driven vessel must keep to a limited area of deep water. In narrow channels keep to the right.

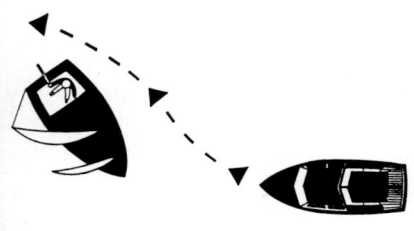

When you have to give way do so in good time, and in a decisive and clear way so that the other vessel's crew can see what you are doing.

Avoid crossing ahead of the other vessel; pass under her stern.

Give way by altering course, reducing speed, stopping or reversing.

EXPEDITIONS AFLOAT

5. **Plan and take part in a half-day's expedition or exercise afloat.**

This is the culmination of the Seaman badge training, and it gives you a chance to put into practice the skills and knowledge you have. Thus the activity is likely to be demanding in the use of boating skills, in the application of safety rules, and in the demands for good seaman-like performance on the water.

Additionally, you must display planning skills. Consider the craft and equipment to be used, and its condition. What about personal clothing and equipment appropriate for your activity, food, the use of maps and charts, contingency plans...?

TRAINING ACTIVITIES

6. **Complete from the list of training activities:**

(a) One item from the Practical Skills section.

(b) One item from the Safety section.

(c) Two items from the Rule of the Road and Communications' section.

(d) A further five items from the remaining five sections.

Advice on these options is given further on in this publication.

The Leading Seaman Badge

Pursuit

1. **Hold the Seaman badge or be at least 13 years of age, and complete requirements 1 to 5 of the Seaman badge.**

Gaining basic skills and knowledge is vital; it increases safety and confidence, and makes it possible for you to do much more demanding and adventurous activities.

PILOTAGE

2. **Have a knowledge of pilotage, navigation lights, sound signals, tides, currents and eddies appropriate to your local waters and activities.**

Local knowledge
This is where you show that you know all you need to about the waters in which you yourself do your boating. Not just theory about boating generally, but your boating in your own waters.

Pilotage
You should know about hazards to navigation, shallows, underwater obstructions, main channels, markers, local light and sound signals, limits of navigation for small craft, places to moor, turn and anchor, weather characteristics.

Navigation lights
After sunset, small craft carry a torch which should be used to help others to see them; it should not be left on continuously. There may be other lights to help you find your way around, and there may be larger craft with proper navigation lights. (Detailed knowledge is not required at this stage.)

Sound signals
These are made by ships to indicate what they are up to.

One blast: I am altering course to starboard.

Two blasts: I am altering course to port.

Three blasts: My engines are going astern.

Five or more blasts: A warning! This is telling you (or someone else!) that you are not taking the correct avoiding action.

One prolonged blast is often used on rivers and in harbours to warn of a vessel's unexpected approach, for instance, around a blind corner.

Tides
You should be aware of the tidal sequences: high, low, spring and neap tides. You should understand the dangers involved with: undertows, overfalls, races and times of particular danger.

Currents and eddies
You should be aware of the dangers associated with: danger spots, effects of weather, eddies which can be used, stoppers.

All this information is available to you locally from clubs, Scouters and water users. They can advise you on the usefulness of publications, of which there are usually a number to be found for most waters. More detailed information connected with these aspects appears elsewhere in this publication.

CARE AND MAINTENANCE

3. **Take care of and maintain a boat or canoe for a period of at least three months.**

All craft must be moored or stored properly, and careful handling ashore is essential. Knocks, scratches and bad support quickly damage boats. It is good practice to leave them clean and dry; this is essential with timber boats.

You must take great care of boats if you are going to enjoy them over a period of years. Always be on the lookout for damage and make repairs as soon as possible. Check buoyancy and toggles in canoes. Maintain ropes, whipping, frayed ends, and replace those which are badly worn. If in doubt, replace. Report damage you cannot fix yourself.

Never put heavy weights in the boat when it is out of water.

On the water, always come alongside gently and without touching if possible. Boat oars and crutches to avoid damage. Use fenders.

At least once a year, give your boat a complete check. Clean and remove mud, stones and other foreign bodies. Smooth down all paint that is flaking. Inspect for signs of damage, cracks, dents, leaks; repair as necessary. Repaint and revarnish.

Keep your boat fully prepared for an emergency.

There is more detailed information later in this publication.

WEATHER

4. **Know how to obtain local weather forecasts, understand their importance and be able to recognise signs of changing weather.**

In your regular activities to date there have probably been adult leaders checking on your progress all the time. To make sound decisions for yourself you need a full understanding of the environment of boating, and that includes weather. If you are going great distances or for a long time, if the water is particularly cold, if your propulsion depends on the wind, if the wind might make it too rough later, your fun could be spoilt, and even change to disaster.

There are many forecasts on radio and television which give some idea of what to expect. Local radio often goes into much greater detail, making it easier for you to interpret.

Another good source for local forecasts is the telephone service. The telephone directory gives details. In most areas dial your local 'Weatherline' and you will get a very helpful pre-recorded local forecast. In most sailing dinghies, winds of force three will be very pleasant for sailing; at force four it will become a little hectic and it may well be better to reef. Even in sheltered waters, force six is normally considered extreme to be out in, and you will need to be well reefed in those conditions. Exposed waters will be much more dangerous because of the build up of swells and heavy seas, and the lack of places with even limited shelter from the wind.

Local features may well affect the weather in one locality, making it more, or less, windy than forecasted, and even affecting the direction of the wind. A sea breeze may add to or subtract from the general wind for the whole sea area. Winds may often follow valleys and rivers, and they may often gust up to twice the mean wind speed. Gusts can often be seen as cat's-paws (dark patches of water) coming towards you.

WEATHER SIGNS

Use your eyes to make better use of forecasts, because what you can see is local weather, what you hear on the radio is a general picture for a large area. Weather usually starts high up in the air. For instance, sometimes on a perfect sailing day you can see clouds very high up moving at high speeds in different directions. This means that there must be winds high up which are likely to reach you soon.

When there are squalls around, gusty conditions are particularly likely. An approaching squall can often be seen by dark clouds and rain. Do not wait until this bad weather reaches you before you seek shelter or reef (or both). The squall may very soon pass over, and you will be able to go out again. Squalls can be seen if you have a view of the horizon. A darkening sky, falling barometer, increasing wind will almost certainly mean worse weather.

Keep a weather eye out. This is the best advice to anyone going on the water. Believe what you can see and do not have blind faith in forecasts.

If in doubt about the weather prospects - do not go! Never put yourself or a crew at danger and do not make it necessary for others to come and help you.

ACTIVITIES AFLOAT

5. Take charge of a party participating in an activity afloat.

Once again, the activity afloat is going to test your good practices as a seaman. Safety and efficiency are essential, and the activity is bound to demand good practical skills.

But there is an additional element; you are now looking after other people. Your leadership skills depend on knowing your stuff as well as many other things. You can only have one skipper in a boat (that's you) and only one person in charge of the activity (that's also you on this occasion). Are all the others acting safely? How can you help them if you need to? Is it clear to all just exactly what you expect? Are certain individuals in need of support?

This activity will be arranged to include some or all the things you have learnt so far, but it should be enjoyable as well as testing your knowledge. It might coincide with your journey to camp or it might just be part of an exciting day on the water.

TRAINING ACTIVITIES

6. Complete from the list of training activities:

(a) One further item from the Practical Skills section.

(b) Two further items from the Safety section.

(c) One further item from the Rule of the Road and Communications section.

(d) A further four items from the remaining five Sections.

Further help is given in the following section of this publication.

The Leading Seaman Badge

MORE BADGES

At this stage of your training, you could well be thinking of taking some other Proficiency badges. Based on the interests you have already covered in this badge, one or two of the following may be suitable.

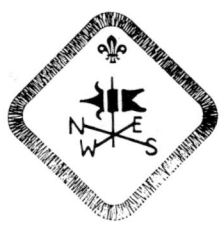

Meteorologist (Pursuit)

Advanced Swimmer (Pursuit)

Navigator (Pursuit)

Boatswain (Pursuit)

Power Coxswain (Pursuit)

Canoeist (Pursuit)

Race Helmsmen (Pursuit)

Helmsmen (Pursuit)

The Master Seaman Badge

Pursuit

1. **Hold the Leading Seaman badge or be at least 14 years of age, and complete requirements 1 to 5 of the Leading Seaman badge, and undertake one item from the Practical Skills section of the training activities.**

When you have completed this badge you should have a general competence at water activities and have a sound skill in at least one specific type of craft. You will have tested skills in leading others afloat and organising water activities, and you will have a good general background knowledge. Even if you have already completed the Leading Seaman badge it is no bad idea to look back at the requirements for all the other Sea Training badges and check that you are well up to standard before you start this final stage.

SIGNALS

2. **Pass a message to another boat or ashore by visual or radio signal, using the correct procedures.**

The most common form of sending signals from boat to shore is by radio telephony, usually using VHF radio. Citizen's Band radio is fairly widely available, and although it is not as strictly controlled as the marine channels on VHF, it still requires some discipline in its use similar to that for marine VHF.

The procedure for marine VHF can be summarised, but it is important that you find out more before using any systems without supervision; there are many more procedures than mentioned here.

Calling is generally done on channel 16. You listen to check that the channel is clear, then with your finger on the transmit button you state the name of the vessel (or shore base) you are calling, followed by **this is** and the name of your vessel twice. Then **over**. They should reply similarly, and direct you to another channel (likely to be channels 8 or 10 if they are another vessel). Each channel has specific functions. You acknowledge (e.g. **going down to eight**) then call them again on the new channel and conduct your business.

Use the radio for as little time as possible; there are many others waiting to use it. When you have finished state **out**, they do the same, and then you return to channel 16 to listen again. Certain stations listen on other channels, for instances many yacht marinas and clubs listen and operate on channel M, and therefore calling on channel 16 is omitted.

Morse Code is still used but not a great deal. The Royal Navy use it (a directed light cannot be intercepted even by satellites), and it is used for radio direction finding. It is easy to set up a system to use this in any other boating situation, but it takes practice to reach a standard which is practical.

The Morse Code					
A	·—	M	——	Y	—·——
B	—···	N	—·	Z	——··
C	—·—·	O	———	1	·————
D	—··	P	·——·	2	··———
E	·	Q	——·—	3	···——
F	··—·	R	·—·	4	····—
G	——·	S	···	5	·····
H	····	T	—	6	—····
I	··	U	··—	7	——···
J	·———	V	···—	8	———··
K	—·—	W	·——	9	————·
L	·—··	X	—··—	0	—————

Rather less common is semaphore, which can still be used as an option, but you will meet even fewer people who can use it.

[Semaphore alphabet chart A–Z]

Remember

Arm, wrist and flag form a straight line.

Move both flags from one position to the next by the shortest possible route.

Only send messages at the rate which you can comfortably receive them.

CHARTS

3. **Have a good working knowledge of charts including projection, datum and symbols used.**

A chart is a map of the sea or coast. There are charts to cover the whole of the world's sea surface. Like maps, charts are produced in various scales. Normally, we use the largest scale charts available.

To read a chart you have to be familiar with the signs and symbols used on them. There are so many of these that there is a special chart, in book form, in which they are detailed. This is chart 5011. There should be a copy of 5011 aboard every large vessel.

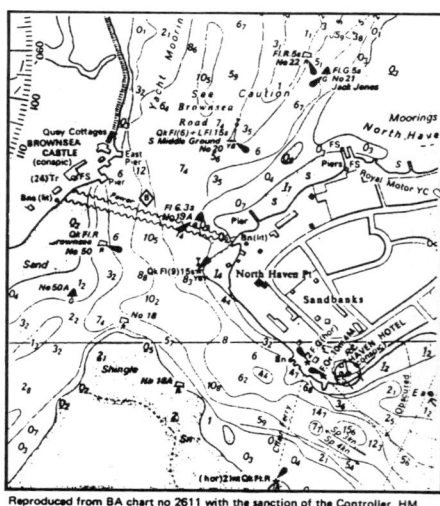

Reproduced from BA chart no 2611 with the sanction of the Controller, HM Stationery Office and of the Hydrographer of the Navy.

Because there is constant change in the details of certain significant features, such as buoys, wrecks and so on, amendments are issued as necessary for all charts. These corrections are published in Admiralty Notices to Mariners and, as the amendments are incorporated, the special space is completed to show that the chart has been brought up to date.

THE COMPASS ROSE

Compass roses appear on the chart - use the one nearest to the area with which you are concerned.

The outer rose is the true compass, the inner the magnetic.

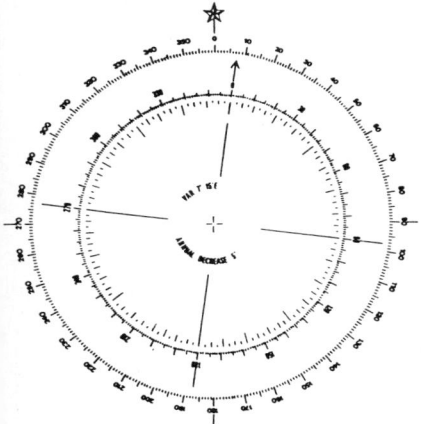

Modern perspex rules can be used to read bearings by moving to any meridian of longitude, or to a compass rose.

When referring to courses and bearings, always use three figures, even if the first is a nought. Thus: 'Zero one five' or 'O one five', 'one seven eight', etc.

See also variation and deviation on page 52.

Chart datum

Chart datum is the height of water below which the sea will be predicted not to go. Thus the depths indicated are the minimum depths which could be expected even at low water springs. However, the depth can be even lower in certain weather conditions, though this is unlikely.

Some contours are marked on charts and show the varying depth of the bottom. Depths are now stated in metres and decimetres. (On old charts, they were given in fathoms.)

Features which are exposed at low tide are marked as 1₃, meaning that the drying height is 1.3 metres above the datum of the chart.

Heights on land are given in metres as the height above the Mean High Water Springs.

One minute of latitude = a nautical mile (1850 metres). The degree of latitude marked on the side of the chart can, therefore, be used as a convenient scale.

Most chart symbols are fairly self-explanatory. The small circle at the base of the symbol shows the exact location of the object (lightship, buoy etc).

Some navigation aids are fitted with coloured lights to make them visible at night. The sequence in which these lights are flashed is indicated on the chart next to the symbol, and the key to the markings is given on chart 5011.

Charts which you use will be on the Mercator projection - like other maps, lines which are straight on these are only approximately so on the spherical world, but they are certainly the best to use. Indeed, you'll never notice any error due to projection.

ACTIVITY RULES

4. **Know the activity rules for expeditions as laid down in *Policy, Organisation and Rules*.**

You are now taking very real responsibility for others, so you must get even the technical details right. Freedom to use the skills you have acquired requires this discipline.

EXPEDITION

5. Take charge of a two day (one night) expedition on the water, with at least three friends, of which at least 12 hours is to be spent under way.

Whether you go by canoe, pulling, sailing or power boat, whether it is on local or distant waters, this project should be demanding as the climax of the **Seamanship Proficiency badges**. You have skills, and this expedition should use many of them, and should be demanding enough for you to learn from the experience.

TRAINING ACTIVITIES

6. Complete from the list of training activities:

(a) One further item from the Practical Skills section, which must ensure that at least two different water disciplines have been covered in the Seamanship badge scheme.

(b) Six further items from the remaining seven sections.

Advice for these follows in the next section of this publication.

Training activities

These form the basis of the optional parts of the syllabus. In some places only general notes are given to indicate the direction and, at times, the required standard, though where practical the text relates to each specific option. A short bibliography is given at the end to help you find out more and there are hundreds more books around. In all sections except Practical Skills, the requirements allow for a further activity of a similar nature and level of achievement as agreed by the Patrol Leaders' Council.

There are eight sections under the following headings:

PRACTICAL SKILLS

BOATS AND CONSTRUCTION

NAVIGATION

ROPEWORK AND TRADITION

METEOROLOGY

RULES OF THE ROAD AND COMMUNICATIONS

SAFETY

EXPEDITIONS

Practical Skills

- Gain The Scout Association B1 Pulling Certificate.
- Gain The Scout Association B2 Pulling Certificate.
- Gain The Scout Association B3 Pulling Certificate.
- Gain The Scout Association B1 Power Certificate.
- Gain The Scout Association B2 Power Certificate.
- Gain the RYA National Powerboat Level 2 Certificate.
- Gain the BCU 2-Star Test (Kayak or Canadian).
- Gain the BCU 3-Star Test (Kayak or Canadian).
- Gain the BCU Safety Test.
- Gain either the BCU Inland or Sea Proficiency Award.
- Gain the RYA National Dinghy or Keel Boat Certificate Scheme Level 2.
- Gain the RYA National Dinghy or Keel Boat Certificate Scheme Level 3.
- Gain the RYA National Dinghy or Keel Boat Certificate Scheme Level 4.
- Gain the RYA National Dinghy Certificate Scheme Level 5.
- Gain the RYA Young Sailors Scheme Start Sailing Stage 1 Award.
- Gain the RYA Young Sailors Scheme Start Sailing Stage 2 Award.
- Gain the RYA Young Sailors Scheme Start Sailing Stage 3 Award.
- Gain the RYA Young Sailors Scheme Red Badge.
- Gain the RYA Young Sailors Scheme White Badge.
- Gain the RYA Young Sailors Scheme Blue Badge.
- Gain the RYA Competent Crew Certificate (practical).
- Gain the RYA Day Skipper/Watch Leader Certificate (practical).
- Gain the RYA National Windsurfing Scheme Level 2 (inland or open sea).
- Gain the RYA Motor Cruising Certificate.

Note:
  BCU stands for British Canoe Union.
  RYA stands for Royal Yachting Association.

PULLING

Larger rowing boats have four or more oarsmen working together, and this is what is meant by pulling.

PULLING IN A CREW - BOAT ORDERS

Rowing is a sport that can be practised and enjoyed by yourself, with one other person, or in a number of larger groups. Like every other kind of activity, if you are taking part with others, you have to follow orders as they are given.

The coxswain is the person who gives the orders and also steers the boat. The stroke, who sits nearest to the coxswain, sets the time or rhythm and, as a member of the crew sitting forward of the stroke, you take your time from the stroke. The bow is that person seated furthest forward.

When you hear	This is what you do.
Sight your oars	Check oars and crutches ready for shipping
Let go for'ard	Bow lets go and replies 'All gone for'ard'
Let go aft	Stroke lets go and replies 'All gone aft'
Ship crutches	Ship your crutch
In fenders	Bring in fender if appropriate
Shove off for'ard	Bow pushes away from mooring
Shove off aft	Stroke pushes away
Out oars Port/Starboard out oars	Whole crew or Port/Starboard oarsmen place oars in crutches ready to pull, blades feathered (parallel to water)
Stand by to give way Stand by	Lean forward, arms and back straight, blades out of the water
Give way together Port/Starboard give way together	Start pulling, following the stroke

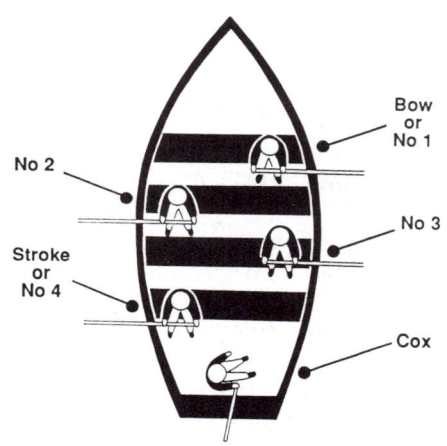

Orders are orders and, in a crew, success depends on everyone understanding what is required of them. Because the progress of the boat depends on the smoothness of the rowing, most orders are obeyed on completing one full stroke after the order is given. Orders should be given when the blades are in the water. 'Hold water', 'Train oars' and 'Mind your oars' are orders given in emergency or hazardous situations and are obeyed instantly.

Initially you only have to know what to do when you hear these orders. Later you will have to be able to given them to your crew!

When you hear	This is what you do.
Mind your oars Mind your port/ starboard oars	Keep clear of any obstruction *Obey immediately*
Back water or Back together. Port/ Starboard back together	Push on the oars instead of pulling, to make the boat go in reverse
Easy all Port/Starboard easy	Reduce pulling rate to slow down or to turn
Eyes in the boat	Pay attention
Trail oars	Trail oars alongside the boat, passing the loom over your head and leaving blade in the water. This is used when passage is restricted and prior to boating oars
Oars	Finish the stroke and complete one further stroke, stop pulling. Sit squarely and upright, oar parellel to the water with blade feathered
Hold water Port/Starboard hold water	Hold or drop your blade in the water at right angles to the surface and keep it steady. This is an emergency order to stop or turn the boat sharply. *Obey immediately*. It is a difficult action and the crew should practise to make it as effective as possible
Gunwale oar	Rest oar athwart the boat and rest on the loom
Toss oars	Only use in double banked boats of large size. Oars are brought smartly to the vertical position by pushing down on the looms, feathered and handles between the feet
Boat oars	Oars placed neatly in the boat, with looms forward in a single banked boat, aft in a double banked boat

STEERING

When the boat is alongside, the bow disembarks and secures the head-rope, stroke disembarks and secures the stern-rope. The coxswain unships the rudder while the crew squares off the oars and gear.

If the boat is steered by a rope operated rudder, the cox holds a rope in each hand, pulling on the starboard rope to go starboard, and the port rope to go port.

The majority of Scout boats will have a wooden tiller connected directly to the rudder. This tiller, kept amidships, will tend to steer a straight course unless it is affected by wind, waves or tide. To go to port, you put the tiller over to the starboard, for starboard, over to port.

Practical Skills

Practical Skills

Remember

Once you have started a boat turning, it will continue to turn, even though you bring the rudder back to midships. Do this just before the boat is heading in the right direction and even ease it slightly over the other way.

A long shallow curve will keep the boat's speed more constant than a sharp turn.

Steering when moving astern is not easy. Move the tiller to port to swing the bow to port; starboard to swing to starboard.

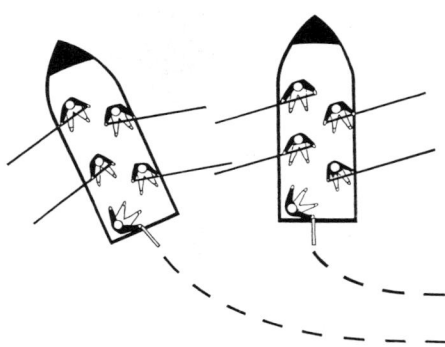

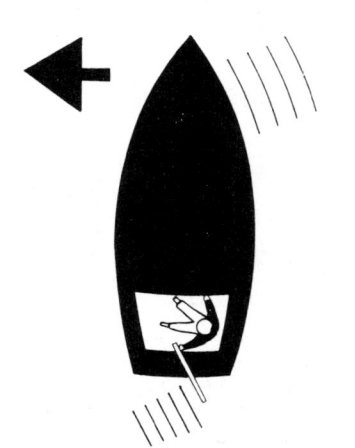

COX A CREW

The coxswain is in charge of the boat, and that means making sure that everything needed is taken, that all equipment is in good shape.

Your checklist:
1. Is the plug securely in its hole?
2. Is there one oar for every crew man and one spare?
3. Is there one crutch for every oar and one spare, all secured by their lanyards?
4. Is there a stretcher for every oarsman?
5. Is the rudder shipped and the tiller secured?
6. Are the painters secured and coiled down?
7. Is the anchor cable secured through the fore ring bolt at the inboard end (if there is no fairlead fitted)?
8. Are bailers and fenders secured by their lanyards?
9. If you are carrying a boat-hook, is it handy to the bowman?
10. Is the lifebuoy within easy reach of the coxswain (that's you)?

The cox is the boss. Keep a firm control on the crew.

Do not allow:

Standing in the boat - unless it is strictly necessary in carrying out an order;
Hands and arms on the gunwales, especially when coming alongside.
Crutches to be left stowed in an unmanned boat;
Remember the pulling orders? Now you have to give them! Have another look at them. Give orders loudly and clearly, following the sequence earlier up to 'Give way together'.

When coming alongside, judge the tide, current and wind carefully, leaving just enough way on the boat so that it drifts into the mooring.

When coming alongside, turn to face the tide.

Turning in a confined space

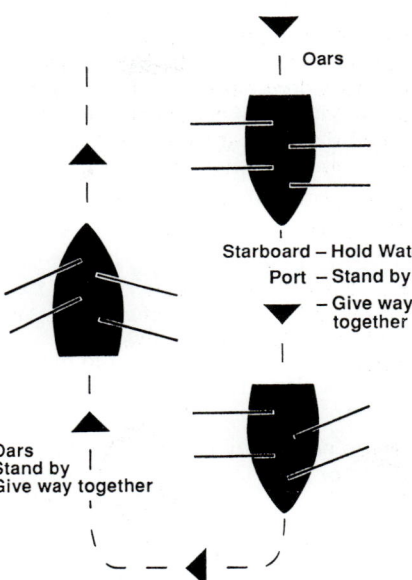

Starboard – Hold Water
Port – Stand by
– Give way together

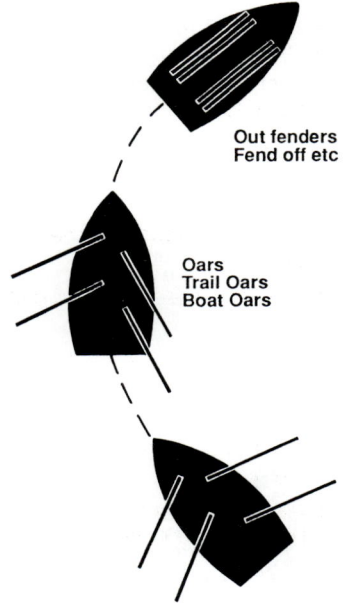

Out fenders
Fend off etc

Oars
Trail Oars
Boat Oars

As coxswain, it is up to you to organise your crew to do the work, which means knowing what you want them to do and telling them to do it at the right time in the right way.

Getting away from an anchorage

The orders will be: 'Ship crutches, out oars'.

(The bow will pull on the anchor cable until it is vertical and shout 'Up and down'.)

You reply: 'Break her out'.

The bow then pulls in the anchor and places it in the bow.

You give the orders, 'Stand by to give way, give way together'.

If the bow is not sure of the precise moment when the anchor cable is vertical, he will not shout 'Up and down', but will wait until the anchor is broken out and shout 'Anchor's aweigh'. On completion of the hauling in of the anchor, the sequence of orders will again be 'Stand by to give way, give way together'.

Picking up a buoy

Picking up a buoy is basically the same manoeuvre as coming alongside. The bow may guide the boat home using a boat-hook if necessary.

The orders are: 'Bow prepare to pick up buoy; easy all; hold water all' (if necessary).

Getting away from a buoy

The orders are: 'Ship crutches, Out oars, Cast off for'ard, Stand by to give way'. Once clear, the order 'Give way together'.

It may be necessary to back off if there is a wind or tide.

Towing a small boat

Approach the boat head to wind and give orders as follows: 'Trail oars', as you approach close enough to reach the boat's painter, which should be secured to the stern of your boat. 'Stand by to give way', 'Give way together'.

The master of the boat that is towing has command of both boats. Decisions must be made as different circumstances arise, i.e. whether to remove the following boat's rudder. If this is not done and crew are left in the boat being towed they should be instructed to steer for the towing boat's rudder at all times.

If a sailing boat is taken into tow, the centre or daggerboard should always be raised as it would otherwise cause the dinghy to yaw widely.

POWER

Power craft are not as easy to handle as many think. To go in a reasonably straight line is simple, but manoeuvring in confined quarters is not so simple. Manoeuvres must be carried out at a safe speed, without damaging property or people.

Some tips ...

Vessels turn sharper circles when going slowly. If a boat is stationary, and the helm is put over before the power is applied, much more turning is achieved. A very short burst of power may start to turn a boat without giving it any headway at all.

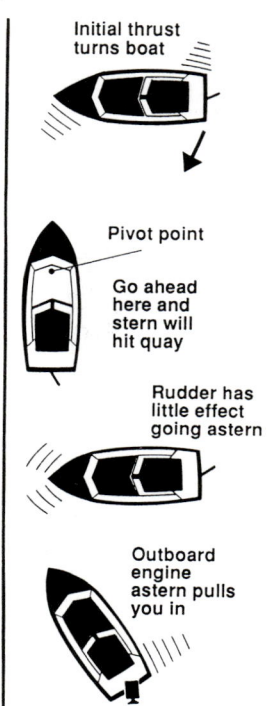

Initial thrust turns boat

Pivot point

Go ahead here and stern will hit quay

Rudder has little effect going astern

Outboard engine astern pulls you in

Inboard engine craft pivot near the bow and, therefore, when you steer to starboard the stern moves well over to port.

The helm has very much more effect when going forwards rather than backwards. You can steer a boat going astern by giving it a short burst of forward power, without actually stopping sternward movement.

Outboards are different in many ways, and you must have received good instruction before attempting to operate a powerful one. You cannot steer without having the power on, and coming alongside may need a touch of power astern to take the way off with the helm reversed to pull it in.

A spring, as illustrated, with suitable fender can be used under low power ahead to swing the stern out to get clear (but beware tides and make sure your fingers do not get caught in cleats or bollards).

Then you can go off astern.

Stopping usually requires putting the engine astern. Then watch carefully and go into neutral as soon as you have stopped.

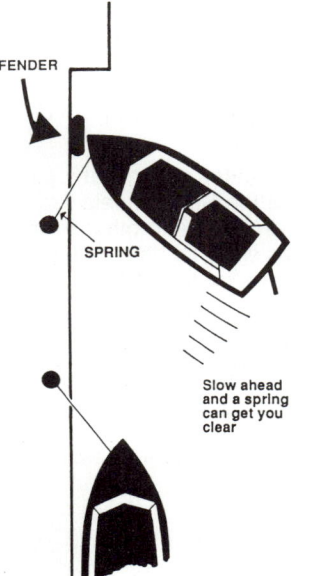

All engines need checking; the fuel level, that the stern gland is tight (the grease filled seal on the propeller shaft), the oil level and that cooling water is flowing after you have started. The instruction handbook will describe routine servicing.

Always remember the special dangers of propellers. Do not go near swimmers unless vital. If you are picking up a person from the water then it is often safer to cut the engines once you have reached the casualty. Ropes must, of course, also be kept clear of the propeller.

CANOEING

To develop your skill you will need instruction in many of the basic strokes and techniques - and plenty of practice! Remember that both the Association rules and the good practice guidance of the British Canoe Union state that canoeing as an activity should be carried out in groups of not less than three. One of you will have to have a Scout Association Authorisation (your Leader will tell you how to get one of these), which will allow you to canoe often, without direct supervision. It may be that your Venture Scout Unit has experienced canoeists who can take you with them, either for an afternoon afloat or on a mini expedition. In this way you can get the practice, the benefit of advice and become more experienced.

A lot of help can be obtained by reading *CANOEING - Skills and Techniques* by Neil Shave, which will give you the correct theory and grounding before you go and practise.

SAILING

We cannot teach you all there is to know about sailing in a small part of a book, but here are some points which will help you.

You will almost certainly get your feet wet when you help to launch and recover the boat and also if you are crew when the boat is brought onto a beach or lee shore.

These are the basic points of sailing.

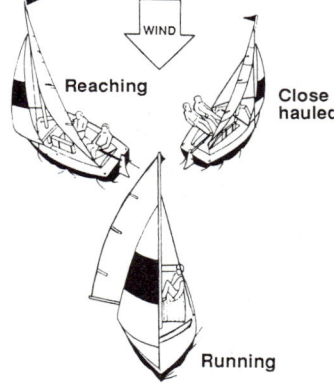

By sailing on simple triangular and figure of eight courses you will demonstrate that you can sail on all points both as crew and helmsman. Consider the five essentials of sailing:

1. **Sail setting.** Sails need to be pulled in as little as is necessary to stop them flapping. As both the wind and your course are liable to change constantly, continual adjustment may be necessary. Do not forget to ease the sheets as you turn away from the wind.

2. **Balance.** The boat will normally sail best if it is leaning just a little away from the wind (to leeward), but only a few degrees. The crew has a special responsibility for balancing the boat by moving into the centre of the boat or even the lee side when necessary, and by leaning right out on the weather side (use the toe straps) at other times to balance stronger winds.

3. **Trim.** The fore-and-aft attitude of the boat. Close hauled boats need the weight slightly forward; reaching and running need it nearer the stern, so the transom is in the water.

4. **Centreboard.** The crew normally adjusts this. Here is some basic guidance.
    (i) close hauled - fully down
    (ii) close reach - three quarters down
    (iii) beam reach - half down
    (iv) broad reach - quarter down
    (v) running - about 15cm of the board protruding

5. **Course sailed.** There are usually many different courses to one point. Think about whether you need to take long or short tacks, to go in deep or shallow water, how to avoid obstructions and other craft which have the right of way.

MORE ON SAILING

RYA Certificates cover many other aspects of the Seamanship Proficiency badges, and relate to other Proficiency badges as well. To obtain details if you want to work for this option, write to:

The Royal Yachting Association,
RYA House,
Romsey Road,
Eastleigh,
Hampshire, SO5 4YA.

(Enclose a stamped addressed envelope.)

Tacking

Tacking means turning through the wind.

Remember

To keep the tiller over until the sail starts to refill.

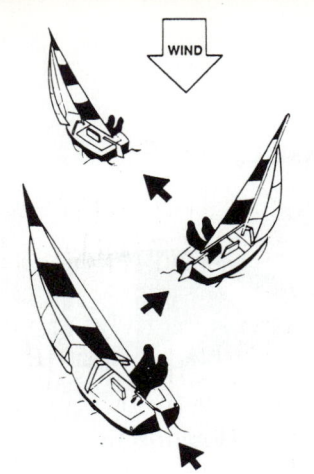

Gybing

Gybing means turning with the wind going round the stern of the boat.

Remember

To centre the helm as the boom comes amidships.

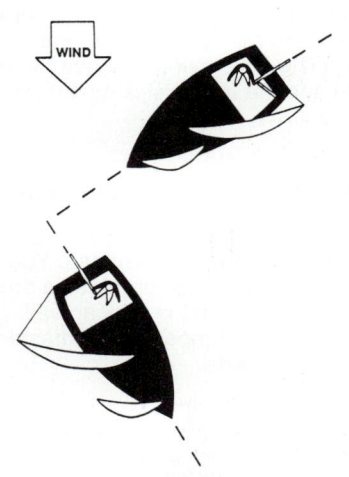

Wearing

Small boat-users usually use the word 'wearing' to mean tacking instead of gybing which is usually done in heavy weather for safety reasons. The advantage of wearing is that the boom changes sides when the sail is empty.

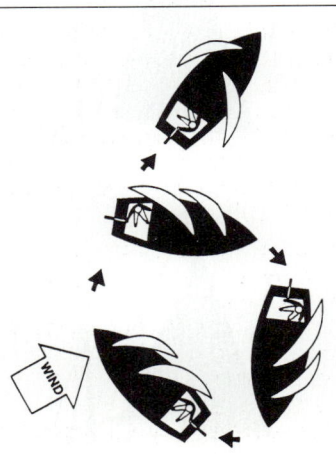

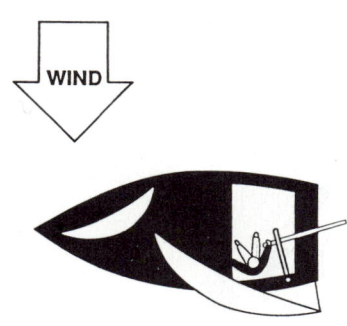

Heaving to

Tasks such as reefing are best done, if under way, by heaving to first. Back the jib and balance the mainsail, rudder and centreboard so that the boat almost stops. (The jib is trying to move the boat astern and the mainsail is moving it ahead.)

Making and shortening a sail

Making sail simply means hoisting the sails into their correct positions. You should also be able to organise a crew to follow your orders in making sail. Leadership is as important as mastering the technical skills.

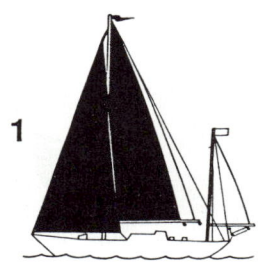

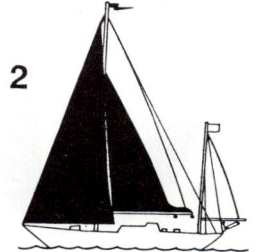

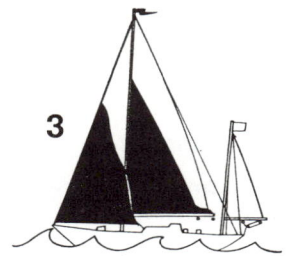

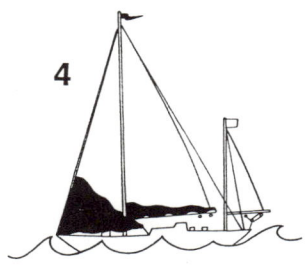

Shortening sail is the reverse - reducing the sail area by taking in one or more sails, or by reefing. If you are in a craft with more than one sail like a ketch or yawl, you can take in the main, leaving a well balanced boat with much less canvas; alternatively you can take in the mizzen, foresail and the jib leaving the mainsail.

Reefing

Reefing means reducing an area of sail. Having too much sail might make life more exciting, but it might also cause quite unnecessary dangers. Boats often sail much better when reefed, even before bad conditions occur. (A reefed boat is also more suitable for instructing in when there is any wind.)

Slacken the downhaul, ease the halyard, ease the boom off the squared portion of the pin and roll the required amount of sail around the boom. Then replace the boom, haul in the halyard and refix the downhaul.

Remember

Always reef or shorten sail in good time – it is always easier to shake out a reef if you find that it is not needed after all.

Getting under way and coming alongside from any direction

The basic technique of getting under way when under sail is the same as that shown in respect of pulling boats. When coming alongside the skill is being able to maintain steerage way for as long as necessary and to stop at the right moment. This is usually done by turning into the wind at the right moment but on a lee shore it may be necessary to come in under the jib only.

Anchoring safely

You may know how to prepare an anchor and the basic technique of anchoring, but there is a great deal to know about this, and all other aspects of seamanship. There are rather different ways of going about it in different circumstances.

When the tide and wind are in similar directions (A).

Luff up into the wind, let go the sheets and, when the way is off the boat, drop the anchor. Pay out at least three times as much cable as the depth of water and bring her up. Finally lower the jib and mainsail. In bad weather it may be necessary to pay out as much as five times the depth of water, provided the boat has room to swing.

Practical Skills

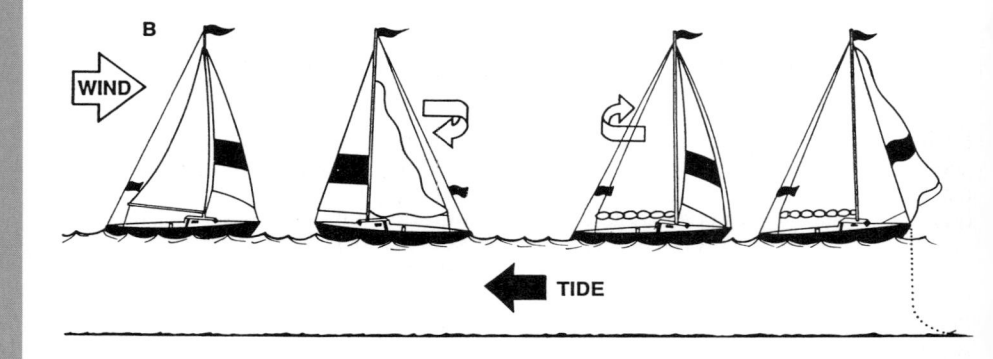

When tide and wind are in opposite directions (B).

Approach the anchor point with the wind behind you, in order to stem the tide. Luff up head to wind then lower the mainsail. Turn at once back through 180 degrees backing the jib if necessary to get out of irons. Run under the jib and let fly the jib. When the tide begins to take you astern drop anchor.

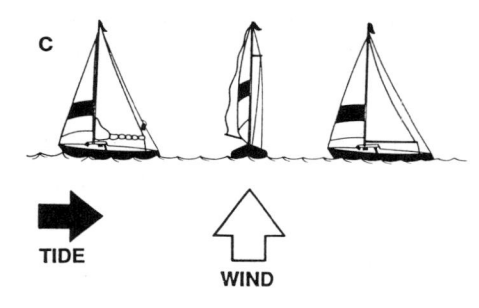

When the tide and wind are at right angles (C).

Luff up into the wind, lower the mainsail, do a broad reach under the jib then let fly the jib and when the tide begins to take you astern drop anchor.

Remember

It is always better to have too much cable than too little.

Sailing up and making fast to a buoy

This is very similar in method to anchoring. You must, however, ensure that you have sufficient way on the craft to reach the buoy but not too much so that you overshoot it. To make sure of this, do not let fly the sheets until you are certain of reaching the target. While it is always desirable to pick up the buoy first time, there is no disgrace whatsoever in abandoning an attempt and coming round again.

Appoint someone to pick up the buoy. This will leave you free to handle the boat. That person can guide you to the buoy and call out when it has been caught.

The chains should then be led through the stem fairlead and secured to the mooring cleat. All remaining sails should be lowered as fast as possible. If you will only be staying a short while at the buoy, reeve your painter as a slip rope from one bow, cleat through the ring on the buoy and back.

ANCHORING

If you are using an Admiralty Pattern anchor, make sure that it is properly stocked. Place the stock centrally through the hole in the shank, insert the forelock and seize it securely with wire.

Check that the warp or chain is attached to the ring.

Tie the rope with a Fisherman's bend or Anchor bend.

Check that the other end of the chain or warp is firmly secured to the boat. Again use a Fisherman's bend or a round turn and two half hitches.

Ensure that the warp or cable is coiled for free running.

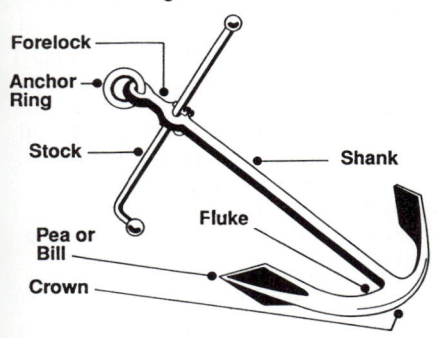

Forelock
Anchor Ring
Stock
Shank
Fluke
Pea or Bill
Crown

Allow a length equivalent to three times the depth of the water at high tide for the cable or warp. If the holding ground is bad or if there are strong winds, increase the allowance by the depth again, providing there is enough room for the boat to swing.

It is better to run out too much cable than too little.

Clay and mud are the best types of ground for holding; sand and gravel are reasonable but shingle or rock is unreliable.

You will have to think about:

   How long you are staying.

   Whether conditions are likely to change.

   How much higher or lower will the tide go?

   Whether you need to leave a watch keeper aboard.

   Is there shelter from wind and sea?

   Is there sufficient swinging room?

   Will you be left aground when the tide goes out?

Make your final approach against the tide. If you are entering a river from seaward with the flood tide, you must turn to face the tide before anchoring.

Take soundings before anchoring so that you know how much cable to pay out. A boathook may be sufficient for this purpose if you are in shallow water.

Stand clear as the cable is running out.

Remember to secure the anchor inboard before you lower the anchor over the side.

The anchor will drop vertically and you should pay out cable as the boat drifts astern with the tide or wind.

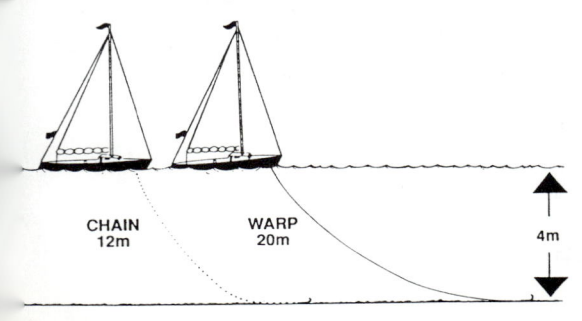

Practical Skills

CHAIN 12m   WARP 20m   4m

Practical Skills

Is the anchor holding?

To find out, fix your position by reference to landmarks. After a minute or two, see if it has changed. If it has, the anchor is dragging. Pay out more cable. If you find on rechecking that you have moved again, up anchor and try somewhere else.

OTHER ACTIVITIES

Offshore sailing, board sailing, dinghy racing and motor cruising are all activities with good training schemes run by the RYA, and many publications are available to support them. There are opportunities to go on courses run by The Scout Association as well as other organisations.

SAFETY

In the water

The **H.E.L.P.** posture is illustrated. The idea is to minimise heat and energy loss, hence **Heat Exposure Lessening Position.**

Help Position

The **'HUDDLE'** position is intended to make people in the water more conspicuous. It can also facilitate the sharing of buoyancy aids (but approach a drowning person with care).

Huddle Position

Lifejackets are worn to keep one afloat and are designed in such a way that even an unconscious person or one unable to help themselves (for instance because of hypothermia) will be able to breathe.

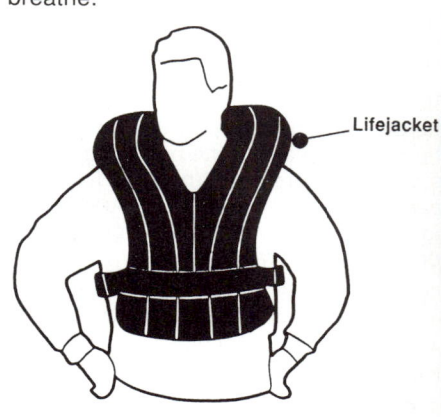

Lifejacket

40

Buoyancy aids, by contrast, only keep one afloat, not necessarily with the face out of the water. So in a situation of possible long exposure in water or injury the lifejacket is essential. This must conform either to British Standard 3595, and have the Kitemark printed on it, or to European Standard and be marked with the EC symbol. They do not have their full buoyant properties until inflated, usually orally. (The Scout Association recommends the use of lifejackets with part built in buoyancy.)

Temperature loss is a killer. The correct clothing can minimise the risks - waterproofs, jerseys and in cold conditions a wet suit. Obviously to stay dry is important, but not always possible. The chill factor is drastically increased by wind. So if you start to get cold, get into the warm. Keep clothes on in the water - they will still help to keep you warm, and conserve your energy. Stay with the boat.

There will still be isolated incidents where individuals get too cold, not just uncomfortably so, but so cold that the temperature of their body core starts to drop. This is very dangerous; symptoms vary, but a lack of will to help oneself, inability to respond, and even a stopping of shivering are signs. Anyone affected must be made dry and moved from the wind. Do not rub them, or give alcohol; both these remove heat from the inner body where it is needed to stay alive. But a hot drink is safe (provided there is no injury which might need surgery). An exposure bag is, therefore, a vital piece of equipment for long passages in open boats. As soon as possible call for help. **COLD CAN KILL.**

Canoe rescue

In conjunction with another canoeist, demonstrate two methods of canoe rescue.

There are many methods of deep water rescue; here are two specific ones which can generally be managed even by fairly small people.

The **rafted X** is done by two upright canoes rafting up, and then one of the canoeists heaves on the inverted canoe, preferably pulling the front up first, until it can be pivoted to empty it. The second canoeist steadies the first so that he can put all his might into it, and the swimmer keeps hold of the paddles as well as holding on to the rafted canoes for his own safety. If necessary he can add extra weight to tipping his canoe while it is inverted.

The **H** rescue is similar, except that the inverted canoe is pulled across the paddles of the two canoes as illustrated.

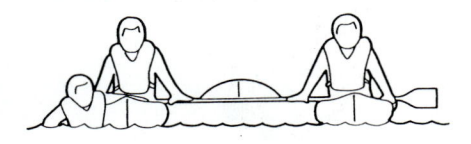

Practical Skills

To finish with, the rescued boat is rafted between the other two and steadied while the swimmer climbs in feet first.

- **Heave a lifeline from a boat, to land within reach of a target eight metres away, twice within three attempts.**

Note: A greater distance is required here than is needed in the Seaman Badge.

RESCUE EXERCISE

- **Acting as an assistant in a rescue exercise, board a stranded craft and bring it ashore single-handed.**

This is to test your initiative in an unforeseen situation, so there's no point in our telling you what to do. Here is the sort of thing that might happen.

You will be taken to a vessel that, for some reason or other, is stranded - it may be a beached dinghy, it may be a sailing vessel with a broken mast. It might be a capsized boat with the gear floating away from it, or a sailing boat with its gear caught up in trees on a lee shore.

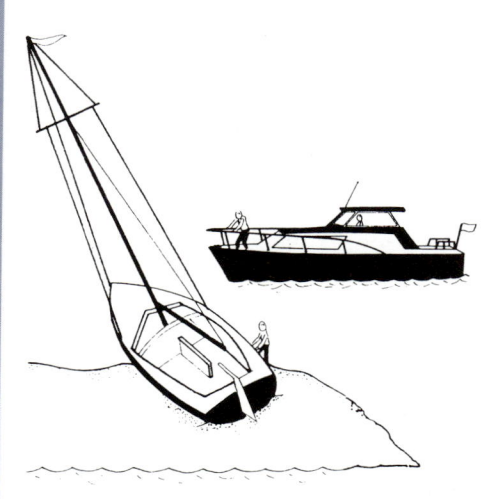

It is your job to see what is wrong and how to put it right, and then get the vessel home. You have to do it, backing your own judgement and ideas with your own action.

MAN OVERBOARD

- **Under sail, demonstrate man overboard drill using a suitable object.**

Imagine that you are one of two people sailing a day boat in fairly hectic conditions and your companion goes over the side. How do you go about picking him up?

The boat will be over canvassed for one, so gybing should be avoided. Instead go on to a beam and sail away from the person in the water until there is room to go about and sail approximately on the other beam reach. Ignore the jib if it is difficult.

Approach the person slowly, keeping the person on the weather side and slacking the sheets to lose way. Do not turn into the wind, but try to keep the wind just ahead of the beam.

Grab the casualty just abaft your weather shroud and help them aboard.

A 20 litre plastic drum, three quarters full of water and attached by about 50cm of line to an empty 2 litre plastic container makes a suitable practice casualty.

- **Using a training manikin, demonstrate the correct method of ventilation.**

It is important that whenever you practise oral (mouth-to-mouth) ventilation you should use a purpose-built model and **never** someone who is already breathing.

Clear the mouth of any loose objects, for example seaweed, false or broken teeth, chewing gum. Make sure the tongue is free of the airway

Tilt the head back, pinch the nose tightly to prevent air escaping and, after taking a deep breath, blow firmly into the mouth.

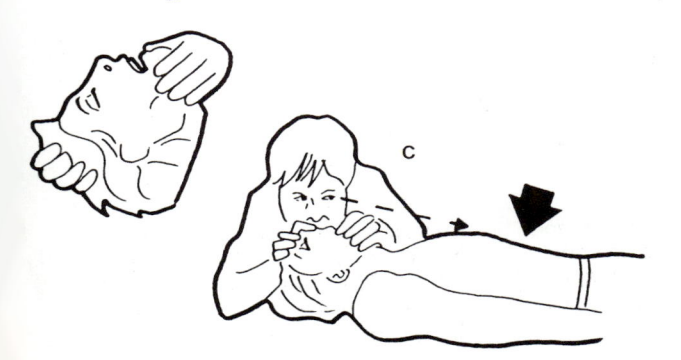

As you blow, watch the chest rising, then move your mouth well away so that you may breathe in a new supply of fresh air.

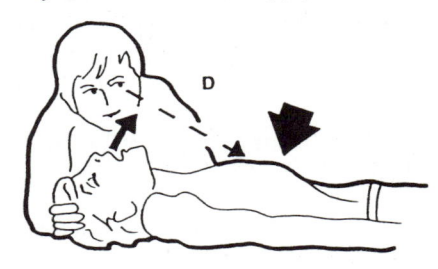

Do not pause during the first four inflations. After that, wait for the chest to fall each time before blowing again. A good guide to the correct breathing rate is to breathe out and then count to yourself ' one thousand, two thousand, three thousand,' then breathe out again and so on.

Recovery position

If someone is unconscious and breathing then they should be put in the recovery position which will help them breathe and prevent them from choking.

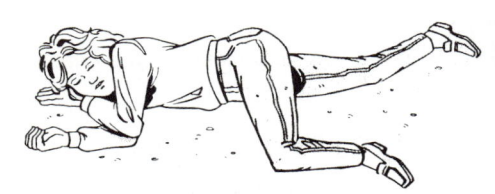

Recovery Position

Practical Skills

Practical Skills

CAPSIZE DRILL

- **Demonstrate capsize drill in a sailing dinghy.**

If your vessel capsizes, you should stay with it, do not try to swim to safety because:

a). If rescue comes before you reach land, the boat can be seen more easily than you can.

b). Distance is deceptive; land is usually further away than it looks.

c). It is difficult to swim whilst wearing a lifejacket.

   DO NOT TAKE IT OFF; you may swim more easily but you can also drown more easily.

d). The vessel has buoyancy; it will support you for as long as you can hold on.

Righting a dinghy

1. Check that the other members of the crew are safe.
2. Helmsman and crew go to the stern and check the rudder and tiller.
3. The helmsman goes to the centreboard, taking the end of the mainsheet as a safety line. (Crew watches to see that the helm gets there.)
4. Crew goes between the boom and the boat, and throws the jib sheet over to the helm. (They can speak to each other through the centreboard case.)
5. Crew lies in the boat (heads forward) so that they are scooped up when the boat comes up.
6. The helm pulls on the jib sheet to right the boat. If necessary the helm may stand on the centreboard close to the hull leaning well back.
7. Crew steadies the boat when it's up and helps the helm aboard.
8. Bail out (or run to shelter/land), plugging the centreboard box if necessary.

If, after three attempts, the boat has still not come up, inflate lifejackets and call for assistance.

Beware of hypothermia. If you are sailing in very cold water, a rescue craft is essential.

Help each other

If you are not alone check that your partner is all right. He or she may be trapped or hurt. A few words from you could be of reassurance.

Trapped in the boat

You may be trapped in a boat - caught in the rigging or in the hull, or under the sail. Keep calm while you sort things out. It is usually reasonably easy to free yourself if you are not panicking. There may be air trapped under the boat which you can breathe anyway. Can you bang on the hull or stick your hand out to call your partner for help?

Practice

You must practise rescue procedures, man overboard drill and capsize drill. You must be confident in the water and under it. You must be used to being in the water wearing a lifejacket or buoyancy aid.

Boats and Construction

- Parts, equipment and preparation.
- Cleaning and painting.
- Repairs under supervision.
- Sail repairs.

These items are dealt with generally in the first part of this section.

BOATS AND THEIR CARE

The list of the parts of a boat always looks daunting, but there is no need to learn the names of the parts by heart. In fact, it would be a bad idea to do so. You need to know why the parts are where they are, what purpose they serve and how they go together. To be able to recite a list of nautical sounding names will serve no useful purpose. So get to know why each part is there, not merely that it is there, and you will learn the names through using a boat. It will not be long before you know them, without realising that you have learnt them.

These are the parts you will get to know.

BOAT REPAIRS

- Under supervision carry out repairs to a boat.

There is no universal repair material, but there are some materials that can be used on most boats. Self-adhesive waterproof tape is obtainable in many widths. This will stick to any smooth dry surface, it can be used in overlapping pieces to cover wider damages. Round corners to prevent curling. If in doubt about the dryness of a surface, wipe it with a cloth soaked in methylated spirit. This tape is particularly useful on plastic coated fabric canoe skins, as the craft can be used immediately after the patch is applied.

There are putty-like sealing compounds which never completely harden. The best known is Seelastik. These can be used to seal cracks, either in the hull or above water. The only glue that can be used on all materials is a two part epoxy, the best known being Araldite. This can be used to join materials. Normal epoxy is slow drying but a quick-setting version is obtainable.

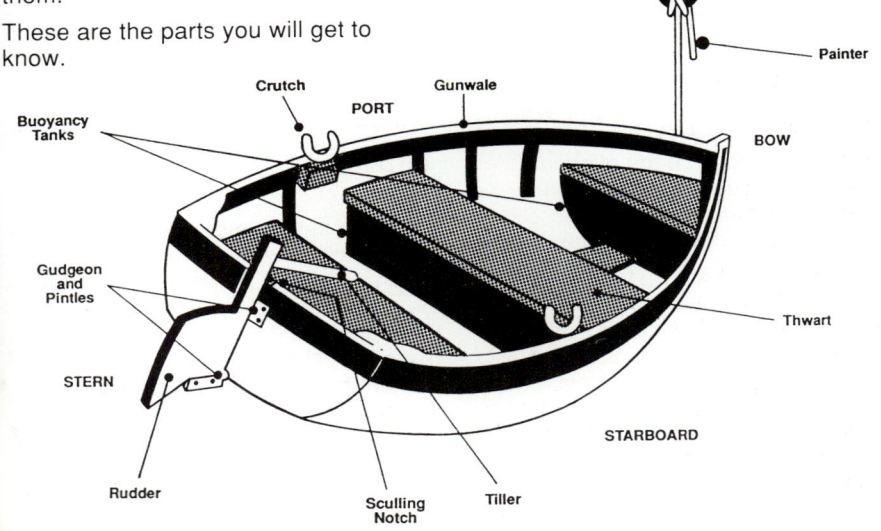

Parts labelled: Buoyancy Tanks, Crutch, PORT, Gunwale, Painter, BOW, Gudgeon and Pintles, STERN, Rudder, Sculling Notch, Tiller, Thwart, STARBOARD

45

Glass fibre

Epoxy glue is probably best to seal and repair minor damage, but for larger damage a repair kit from a minor sundries firm or a glass fibre supplier is best.

The outer surface of a glass fibre boat is protected by a thin resin gel coat. If scratches penetrate this, water can enter and spread through the glass fibre. If there is general wear that penetrates the gel coat, the best treatment is several coats of polyurethane paint. Ordinary paints are unsuitable for glass fibre.

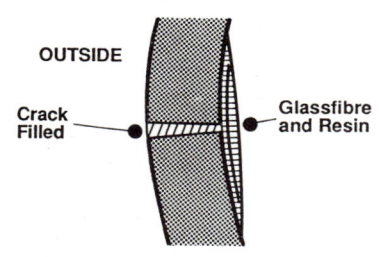

OUTSIDE
Crack Filled
Glassfibre and Resin

Scratches that go deep should be scraped out with a pointed tool. Mix resin to the maker's instructions. Put a few strands of glass fibre in the crack, if there is room, and apply the resin with a brush. Allow the resin to stand above the surface slightly. When it has hardened, sand it flush with the surrounding surface. Most resins will not set at very low temperatures. The kit instructions will tell you the minimum temperature. If you are working on a near vertical surface there are thixotropic resins that will not run.

If the crack goes through, thoroughly sand for an inch or two around it on the inside. Cut a piece of chopped strand glass fibre mat, with scissors, to the size of the sanded part. Mix resin and paint a coat on the inside. Put the mat over this and thoroughly 'wet it in' by using more resin on the brush with a stippling action. You will be able to see when the glass fibre is thoroughly soaked. Leave this to set, then fill the crack on the outside, as described for the simple crack. If the damage is larger, cut away with a hack-saw blade until you have an opening bordered by sound material.

The edge need not be straight or the opening square. Trim the edges with a file. If the skin is thin, bevel slightly towards the inside. If it is thick enough to allow it, make double bevels.

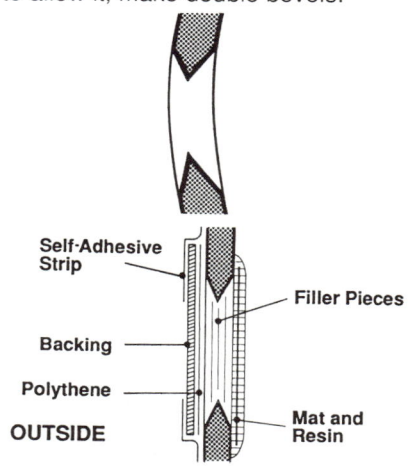

Self-Adhesive Strip
Filler Pieces
Backing
Polythene
OUTSIDE
Mat and Resin

If this is a flat or moderately curved part and the inside is easily accessible, fasten a piece of polythene sheet over the outside with a backing of card or hardboard, held with self-adhesive strip. If it is a small boat that can be tilted, turn the hull so the patch is downwards and near level. Sand an inch or so round the inside. Brush on a coat of resin to cover the polythene, worked close to the cut edge. Let this dry until sticky. Cut glass fibre to fit in the opening. If you have woven cloth use it, but most repair kits only have the random chopped strand mat. Stipple this in with more resin. Make up the thickness with more layers and finish with an overlapping layer inside. Remove the polythene when the resin has set.

Complete Inside First

If there is much curve or it is difficult to work from the inside, the inside over-lapping piece may be fixed first. As it gels it may have to be manipulated to follow the shape as near as possible. When this has set, build up from outside with mat or cloth, but make sure the outer surface is resin only without strands of glass coming through. The outer surface can only be made approximately true, although something can be done by pressing polythene against it before it hardens. If the outside finish is important the patch will have to be sanded, then it can be polished with a scouring powder followed by a polishing paste. However, it is unlikely that the colour of the patch will match, and the best treatment is to paint the hull with polyurethane paint. Of course, you should wear gloves when making this kind of repair.

Note: Precautions should be taken when using glass fibre, glass mat and resins. Work in a well ventilated space, follow the manufacturer's instructions, keep clear of naked flames and use safety goggles and gloves.

Plywood

Small damage can be sealed with epoxy or other waterproof glue mixed with sawdust and pressed in. Glue without sawdust may craze as it sets and leak slightly. Larger damage may be trimmed around, or a square and a slightly tapered block of solid wood glued in. Trim the outside flush after the glue has set.

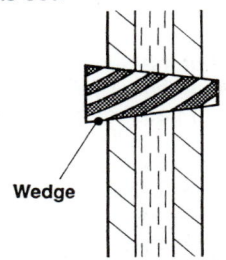

Wedge

Slightly larger damage is better dealt with by trimming to a regular shape and fitting in another piece of similar plywood, with a similar piece behind it. This is best done in two stages. Clean paint or varnish from around the inside of the cut out. Make a backing piece, preferably with bevelled edges and rounded corners and glue this in. If possible, hold it with weights or a strut, but if this is impossible use thin brass shoe nails. The points can be cut off later. When this glue has set, glue in the patching piece.

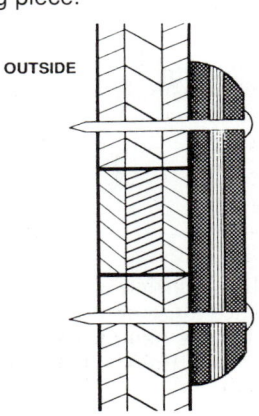

OUTSIDE

Boats and Construction

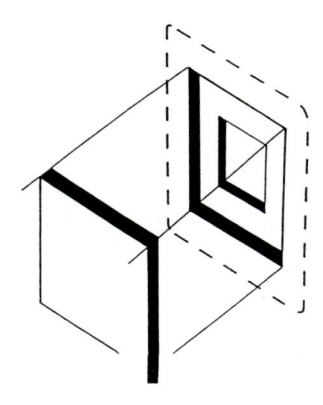

If the damage is larger or much curve is involved, cut out the centre of the backing piece to make a frame. This will allow cramps to pass through and pull it to the shape of the hull while the glue sets. If a full-thickness piece of plywood cannot be pulled to the curve, make up the patching piece with two thinner parts. Brass nails may have to be used through the patch.

Timber

The usual damage to a wooden hull involves a patching plank. The professional method involves replacing part of the plank, but an emergency repair is made with a tingle. This is a patch put on the outside. For a clinker boat, cut a piece of wood large enough to cover the damage and fit against the plank above.

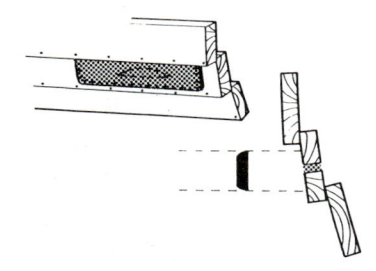

For the flush planking of a curved hull, make a patch large enough to cover the damage. It looks neatest if it follows the lines of a plank. Bevel off all exposed edges (fairing off).

Coat the underside of the tingle with jointing compound (Seelastik). Put more on the damage, if necessary. Fix the tingle down tightly on this. Traditionally canvas and plenty of paint was used, but the jointing compound makes a better job and is cleaner. How the tingle is fixed depends on the planking. If it is thick enough, use brass screws, sufficiently close to pull the joint tight.

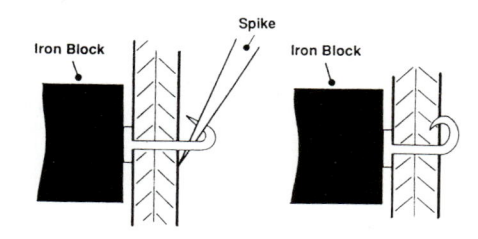

Galvanised nails can be used, driven through and clenched. Drive each nail through the tingle and plank. It may be advisable to drill an under-sized hole first. Get someone to hold an iron block against the nail head. Inside start bending the nail end over the point of a spike, then drive it into the wood. It is stronger if driven diagonally to the grain.

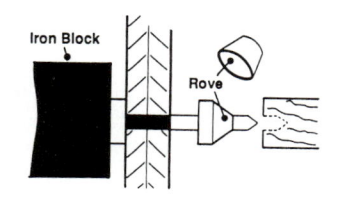

Copper nails and roves (conical washers) are the best way of fixing a tingle. They will probably have been used in construction.

Copper boat nails are square and the matching rover has a hole just too small to press over the nail. Drill a hole for each nail and drive it from the outside.

With the head supported, drive a rove over the point with the end grain of a piece of wood, or a hollow punch. Cut off the end of the nail a short distance above the rove, with end cutting pliers.

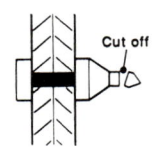

With a ball or cross hammer rivet the end over the rove, using light strokes to avoid buckling the nail in the wood.

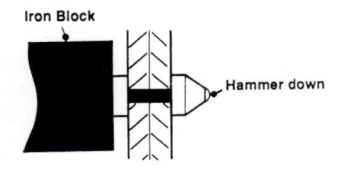

In a boat with bent frames or timbers some of these may crack as the boat works, an occasional broken one does not matter, but if there are several, they should be repaired. In some cases it is advisable to replace a timber completely but in most cases it is satisfactory to double up. This is done by putting a short piece of similar timber alongside the damage.

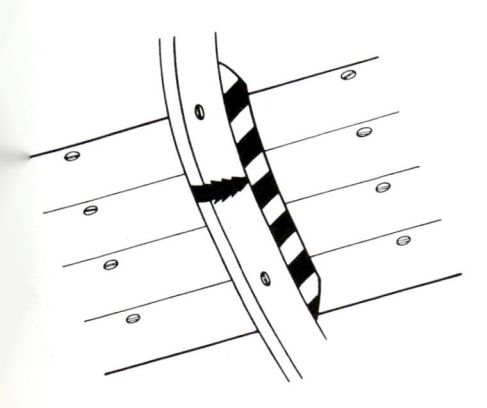

If it can be sprung to shape and held there it is fixed by using copper nails and roves through it and the plank overlaps. If there is too much curve to allow easy bending, the doubling piece may be laminated from two or more thinner pieces. These are prepared, then pushed into place on top of each other with wet waterproof glue between and riveted before the glue has set.

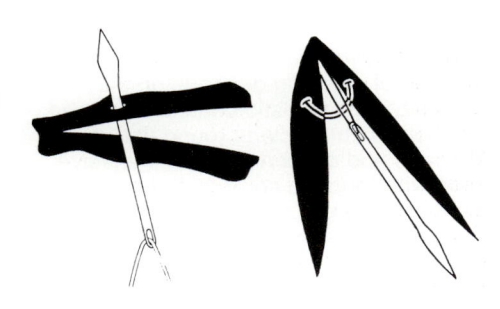

Fabric

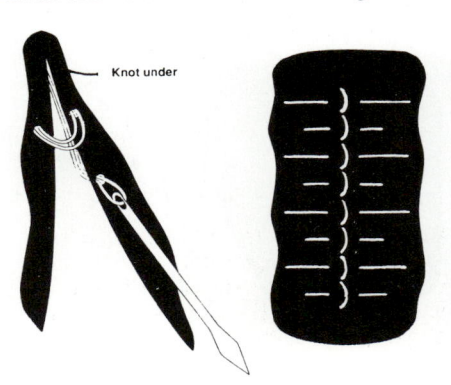

A boat repairer may have to deal with torn sails or damage to a fabric-covered canoe. A small tear in a sail can soon develop to a larger one, so it should be dealt with at once. The thread used should be sail twine or stout Terylene thread, with a triangular-pointed sail needle, about size 16. If there is much sewing to be done a sailmaker's palm is advisable to push the needle through. A small tear is closed with a herringbone stitch. Have the thread doubled and the end knotted together. Push the needle up through the far side of one end of the tear, then go down through the far side and let the needle come up to the left of the stitch. Crossover the stitch and up the far side again. For a torn sail, keep the stitches as close together as possible and make them of different lengths. In this way the cross-over parts of the stitches will fill the space, making a patch unnecessary.

If a fabric covered canoe is holed the method of patching depends on the material. If it is plastic-coated fabric and the hole is small, clean round the damage and cover it with self-adhesive tape with rounded corners. If the damage is larger, pull the edges together, either with widely spaced herringbone stitches or simple zig-zag stitching.

This may be covered with a self-adhesive strip or a patch made with a similar material to the hull. The adhesive will have to suit the hull, but for most plastic fabrics an impact adhesive, such as Clear Bostik is suitable. If the canoe skin is painted canvas, scrape or sand the paint around the damage to expose canvas fibre.

Sew the edges together and make a canvas patch. Most plastic adhesives are suitable for canvas, but a rubber compound, such as Black Bostik will do.

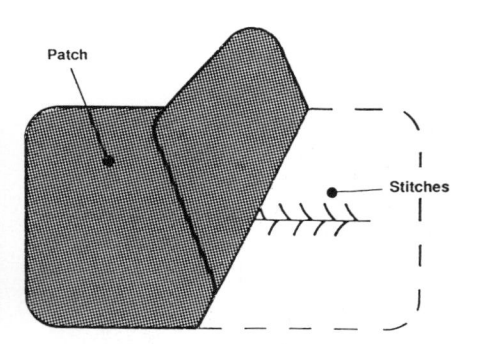

RIGGING A SAILING BOAT

- **Rig a sailing boat and name the parts of the gear.**

Rigging a boat is practical, and you need practical instruction to do it, initially dealing with one particular type of boat.

Many Scout boats are dual purpose vessels, and are kept with the mast down. The first thing you must learn, therefore, is to be able to rig the mast.

The mast is held in position by the forestay and a shroud on each side. This is called standing rigging.

Running rigging is used to hoist the sails.

Fix the foot of the mainsail to the boom. This is done by sliding the rope sewn along the foot of the sail into a groove in the boom, placing slides into a track and simply tying the clew to the after end of the boom.

The tack should now be made fast to the fore end of the boom by the fitting provided and the foot of the sail should be stretched by the clew overhaul. It has to be pulled fairly tight and finished off with a couple of half hitches.

Next, the battens are inserted completely in the batten pockets. Make sure that the sail is not twisted and then fix the headboard by the shackle to the main halyard. The luff of the headboard is slotted into the groove or track in the mast. Make sure the boat is head to the wind when raising the mainsail by pulling the main halyard. The boom is now fitted to the gooseneck and the halyard pulled tight and made fast on the cleat on the mast.

When the mainsail is up, the jib is hoisted. The jib is the smaller sail between the forestay and the mast. Secure the tack to the fitting provided on the stern and clip the luff hanks to the forestay. Fix the head to the jib halyard by the shackle provided. Attach

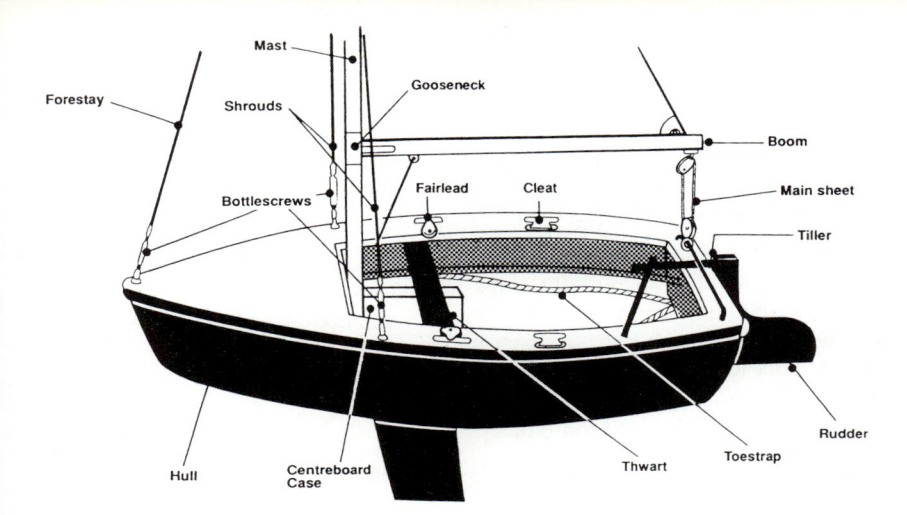

Diagram labels: Mast, Forestay, Shrouds, Gooseneck, Bottlescrews, Fairlead, Cleat, Boom, Main sheet, Tiller, Hull, Centreboard Case, Thwart, Toestrap, Rudder

the jib sheets to the clew and run them through the fairleads. Tie each of the free ends off with a figure of eight knot. Finally haul on the halyard until the luff is taut.

- **Build and maintain a canoe or boat.**
- **Under supervision carry out routine maintenance on an outboard motor and demonstrate the proper fitting to the transom of a boat.**

You will need to find an expert to instruct you in these options.

JURY RIG

A jury rig is a temporary arrangement of masts and sails designed to get you out of trouble. It is impossible to lay down set standards as your approach must be a) practical and b) based on the equipment available. The exercises are designed to stretch your resourcefulness and ability to mix together a wide range of boating skills and experience.

BOSUN'S BAG

This is a bag which will hold tools, materials and spare parts which are likely to come in handy for running repairs and maintenance. If you are going to be able to carry enough of these to make it worthwhile then

obviously the bag has to be fairly large. We suggest that a bag 38 x 45 centimetres will probably be sufficient.

Use No 7 canvas for strength.

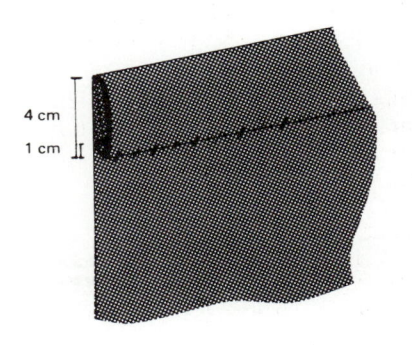

Cut the canvas to a length of 1 metre and a width of 44 centimetres.

Make a hem at each end of 4 centimetres with an extra 1 centimetre tucked under.

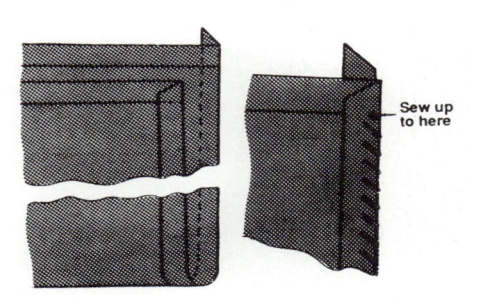

Sew up to here

Boats and Construction

51

Navigation

Fold the hemmed canvas in half and turn back 3cms on each side. Sew the two halves together as far as the hem.

Now cut down the unsewn edge to the hem and sew round the ends of the hem (to stop them fraying).

Thread two cords through both seams and splice them together at each end.

Pull the spliced cords and the bag will close. Pull the other ends and the bag will open.

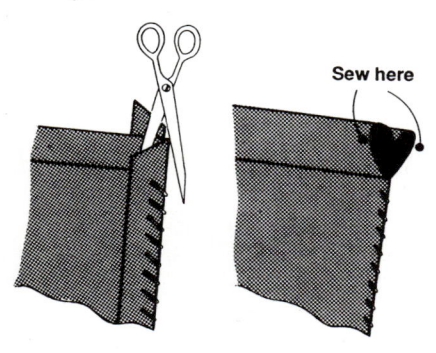

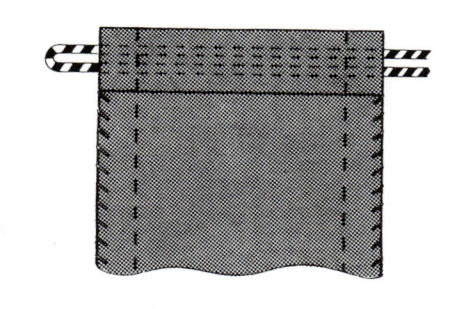

Sew here

- **Build and demonstrate a working model of a boat.**

You may use your own plans, other people's or kits to do this. However, kits must in themselves be demanding or you will need to back your achievement with detailed technical understanding of the design.

Navigation

- **Read a mariner's compass and have a knowledge of variations and deviation.**

A mariner's compass has a circular card marked in degrees which rotates, rather than a simple needle. You can read the heading or bearing by seeing what number is lined up against the **lubber line**. North is 000 degrees (or 360 degrees), and readings are clockwise in degrees. For instance, south-east is 135 degrees.

VARIATION, DEVIATION AND COMPASS ERROR

Compasses point to the magnetic north pole, but the position of this varies from year to year and does not coincide with the North Pole. So, the angle between true and magnetic north will vary from place to place and will change from year to year. In order to use your chart, you therefore need information about the relation between true and magnetic north at the time the chart was drawn. This information is given across the diameter of the compass rose as, for example, *Variation 8 degrees W (1975) decreasing about 9 minutes annually.* This means that in 1975, in relation to the area of the chart, magnetic north was 8 degrees west of true north and that the difference will decrease each year by about 9 minutes. So, we can calculate that in 1976, the difference was 7 degrees 51 minutes; in 1977, it was 7 degrees 42 minutes.

Deviation is the alteration in reading caused by the material of which the vessel is made. It is therefore particular to each vessel and to each course taken by the vessel.

Variation and deviation have to be combined to produce what is known as compass error. If the deviation is 5 degrees east and the variation 7 degrees west the compass error will be 2 degrees west. If the deviation is 5 degrees west and the variation 4 degrees west, the compass error will be 9 degrees west.

If the compass bearing is 45 degrees and you have worked out the compass error as 9 degrees west, deduct the error to find the true course, which will be 36 degrees. If the compass bearing is 45 degrees and the compass error 3 degrees east, add the error to give 48 degrees as the true bearing.

- **Demonstrate how a position may be found by two bearings.**

Details of this are contained in the section on Plotting a Position on page 59.

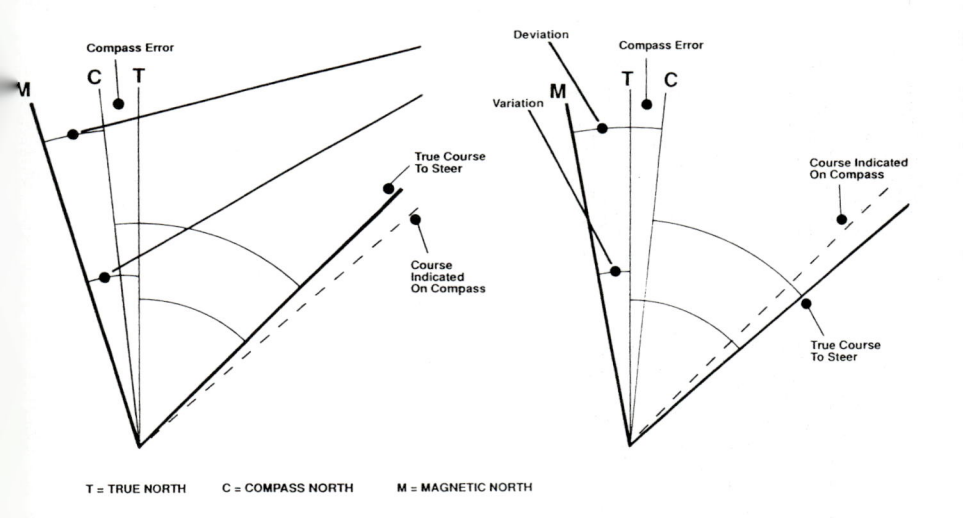

T = TRUE NORTH   C = COMPASS NORTH   M = MAGNETIC NORTH

Compass Error West

Course indicated		45°
Variation	7°W	
Deviation	5°E	
Compass error		2°W
Course to steer		43°

Compass Error East

Course indicated		45°
Variation	5°W	
Deviation	7°E	
Compass Error		2°E
Course to steer		47°

MORE ABOUT TIDES

Tides move outwards from the ocean centre in much the same way as ripples travel outwards in a pond. The tides which affect the British Isles start in the mid Atlantic. They divide at Land's End and travel round the mainland one way by way of the Channel and the other way by way of the Irish Sea.

The part which travels by way of the Channel only gets as far as Harwich, where it meets the previous tide which has travelled all the way round the coast of Scotland and down the east coast of England.

Tides occur differently in different places. The Mediterranean has no noticeable tides, whereas Southampton has two high tides between each low tide - effectively a two hour stand at high water.

Generally, narrow straits and prominent headlands cause the tidal stream to accelerate, often leading to dangerous waters.

Weather conditions also affect tides. Heavy rains will swell rivers. Gales, all coming from the same direction over a long period, will raise the level of water in front of them. Pressure will also raise or lower sea level.

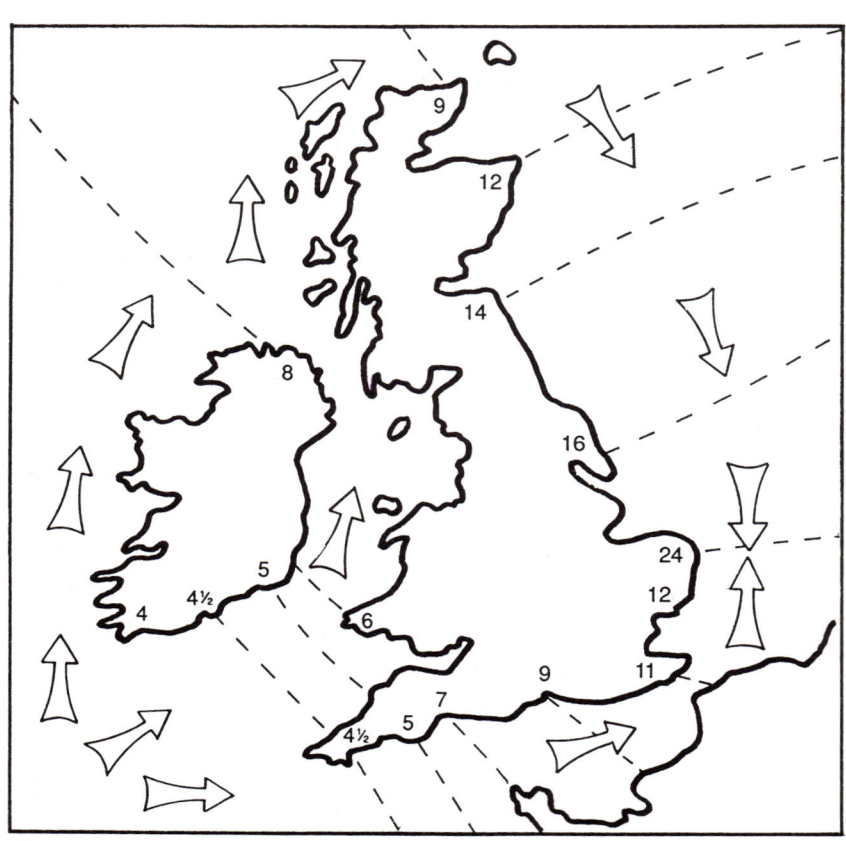

Figures show hours from origin of tide wave

The rate of rise and fall of the tide is not uniform. Very roughly over a six hour period, the rise or fall will follow this pattern:

In the first hour 1/12th of the range
　　　second 2/12ths
　　　third 3/12ths
　　　fourth 3/12ths
　　　fifth 2/12ths
　　　sixth 1/12th

Remember to allow for the swiftest tidal activity when you are anchoring or birthing.

Which way is the tide flowing?

You can tell by:

Ships riding at anchor - they head into the stream.

Buoys - they lean or cant, in the direction in which the tide is moving.

Moored objects - look at the wake.

Demonstrate the use of tide tables and tidal stream atlases.

Note that some tables give only times of high water, others give both high and low water times (occasionally just low is given). Where both are given they normally give the height of the tide, and from those you can tell which are high and which are low.

Times are normally given in Greenwich Mean Time (GMT); if so, during the summer you need to add an hour for British Summer Time (BST). You must use tables for the right year.

Spring tides, which are much stronger, are found by seeing when the heights of high water are particularly high.

DEFINITIONS

Mean sea level – The point between high water and low water or the average sea level.

High water - The highest level to which the water will rise when the tide is coming in.

Low water - The lowest level to which the water will fall when the tide is going out.

Mean High Water Springs (MHWS) and Mean High Water Neaps (MHWN) - The average height of water at the spring and neap tides.

Mean Low Water Spring (MLWS) and Mean Low Water Neaps (MLWN) - The average height of low water at the spring and neap tides.

Navigation

HIGH WATER
FIRTH OF CLYDE GREENOCK
Lat 55° 57' N Long 4° 46' W

G.M.T. ADD 1 HOUR. FOR B.S.T.

Navigation

Tidal stream atlases show the flow of water relative to the time of high water at some major port. The sample page shows the tidal streams two hours after High Water Dover. The whole atlas consists of 13 maps, showing the tides from 6 hours before high water to 6 hours afterwards. In the example given the numbers indicate the strength of tide in tenths of a knot during neap and spring tides. For instance, 27,65 means 2.7 knots at neap tides at 6.5 knots at spring tides. Such atlases are available covering all UK waters.

This information enables you to plan journeys so the tide helps you. You are unlikely to be able to plug a foul tide. Wind against tide makes it rough, therefore you can also anticipate changing sea state.

You can also work out at what angle to steer to cross a tideway, although the information is not usually very accurate close inshore. The example drawn gives an idea of how it is done, for the more mathematical amongst you! The intended real course line and tide lines are drawn first, then the actual steering line assuming a particular speed.

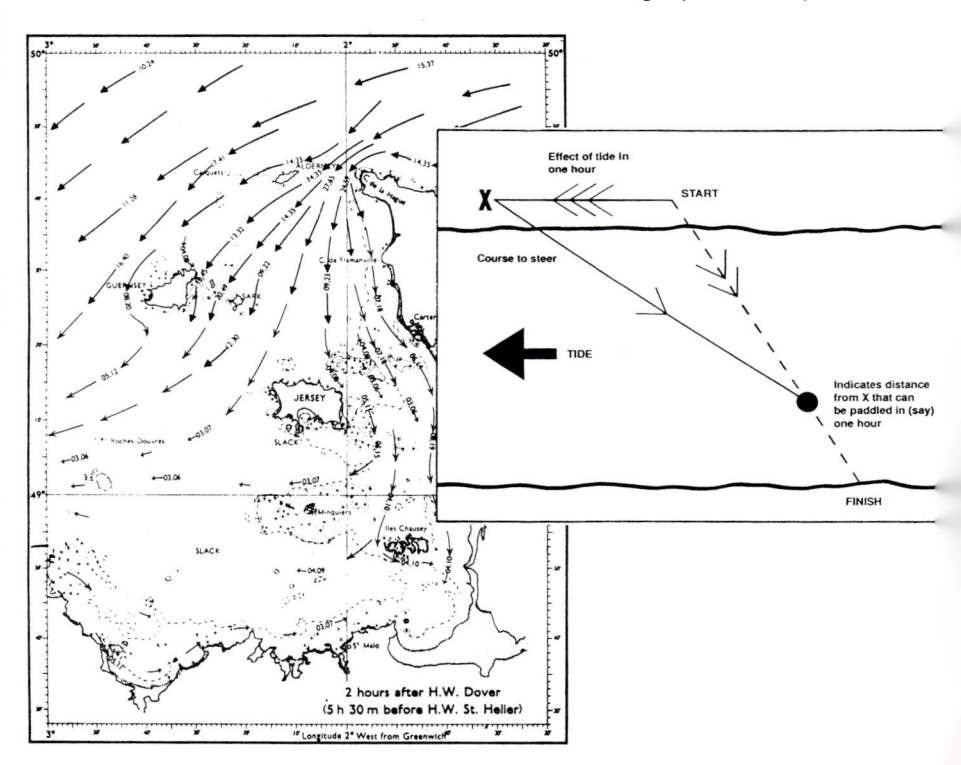

56

- **Explain the system of strip maps of canals and rivers. Use one of these charts to plan an expedition.**

These maps view linear waterways in a way which is very easy for river users to use, showing the main features on and beside the water, but with no strict sense of compass bearing. The example below illustrates this.

As well as using such a map, there is always the possibility of making a sketch map using the same ideas. This could be a worthwhile project, and would act as a good discipline for gaining knowledge of the waters which you use. Other Scouts may well find your efforts useful.

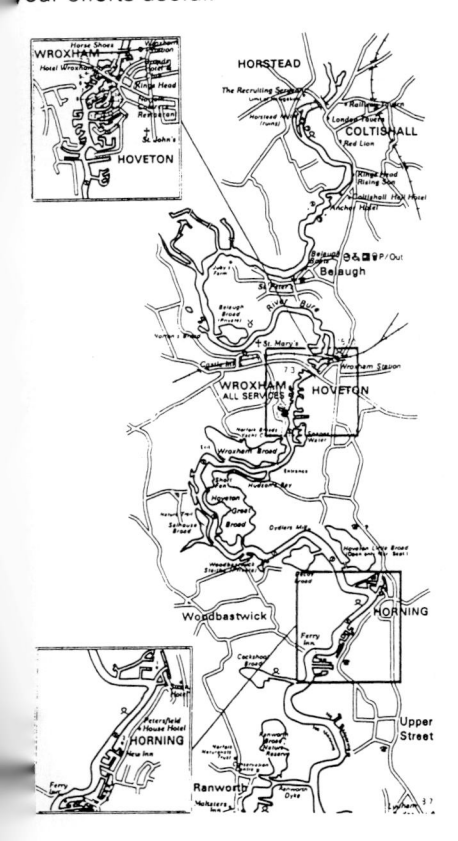

- **Demonstrate how compass error can be found from a transit bearing.**

Sailing any distance on a compass bearing obviously requires a clear knowledge of how accurate the compass is. You have probably met *variation* in compass work ashore; this is compass error due to the difference between magnetic north and true north. Another error occurs because of ferrous metals and other very weak magnetic fields, this is called *deviation*.

If your vessel is lined up with transits (as illustrated) then you can tell from the chart very accurately what its true heading is. Comparison with the steering compass reading gives you the total error. If, for instance, the compass is deflected 10 degrees to the west, then we say it is an error of 10 degrees west. If, on the other hand the compass error were 1 degree east and we knew that there was a variation of 6 degrees west, we would know there is a deviation of 7 degrees east. Hopefully your check will show that there is little or no deviation. But beware, deviation is different on different courses.

Navigation

PLOTTING A POSITION

- **Plot your position using a Decca or satellite navigation system.**

There is a great deal of equipment on the market which makes use of radio signals for navigation. If you are lucky enough to have the opportunity to cruise in an offshore vessel you almost certainly have a chance to use some of this equipment, and it seems a reasonable assumption that the skipper of the vessel will be able to instruct you. The sophistication of different apparatus varies and it is obviously not practical to describe all types in detail. But here are some ideas of what is generally expected.

Radio Direction Finding (R.D.F.)

This involves tuning the set to the correct frequency as published in nautical almanacs. Some sets have digital tuning which makes this easy, but many older ones are difficult as tuning methods are cruder and you may have to tune to a weak intermittent signal, identified by Morse code. Usually a number of distant stations transmit their signals sequentially so that you can follow them round. Each starts with its call sign a few times in Morse code, then gives a prolonged **dash**, and within the minute finishes with its call sign again. Then the next takes over. You have to home in on the **null**, where the signal is weakest during the transmission and find the compass bearing. Even just one reasonable bearing may help you find your position, or at least decide which way to steer.

Some R.D.Fs are more automatic, and some give bearings relative to your course rather than in terms of the compass. Aeronautical beacons are sometimes used, and the sequence of signals is different for these.

The bearing then has to be transferred onto the chart to give your position line.

DECCA and Satellite Navigation systems are becoming more popular in yachts and other small boats. Both are derivatives of the older RDF systems with a much greater degree of accuracy. Though easy to use simply to find a position, you would be expected to be able to set up these devices from when they are first turned on, and programme in waypoints and the like.

There are other systems and more may be developed but these are the most popular in U.K. waters.

You may, of course, combine data from radio systems with other systems to get a position. Then you have to transfer the bearings or latitude and longitude to the chart.

RADAR is another system. If you use this option you will be expected to understand what all the different controls do, how to use the different scales and how to work out bearings and transfer them to a chart. It is often not as easy as it sounds to relate the picture you see to what is around you because of signals reflected back from rough water and because of shadows.

- **Plot your position at sea. Understand the cocked hat principle.**

Compass bearings

This is the most usual way of plotting a position. Using a hand bearing compass take bearings on three objects marked on a chart. Convert these bearings from magnetic bearings by subtracting westerly variations (the number of degrees of westerly variation is indicated in the compass rose on the chart), and draw them on the chart using parallel rules.

Parallel rules can be used in two ways. Either walk them to one of the compass roses or (with modern perspex ones) walk them to any meridian of longitude, close them, and read the bearing.

You might expect the three bearings to pass through one point (your position) but due to errors they will almost certainly form a triangle (called the cocked hat). You take your position to be the most dangerous point in the triangle. If you can only get two bearings they will give you a fix, but a third bearing may indicate a mistake if you have made one.

The bearings you take give you position lines - lines along which you know you are. There are many other ways of finding position lines. Any two intersecting position lines give you a fix, and a third one acts as a check. Here are some of the other position lines.

Transits

When two objects are in line.

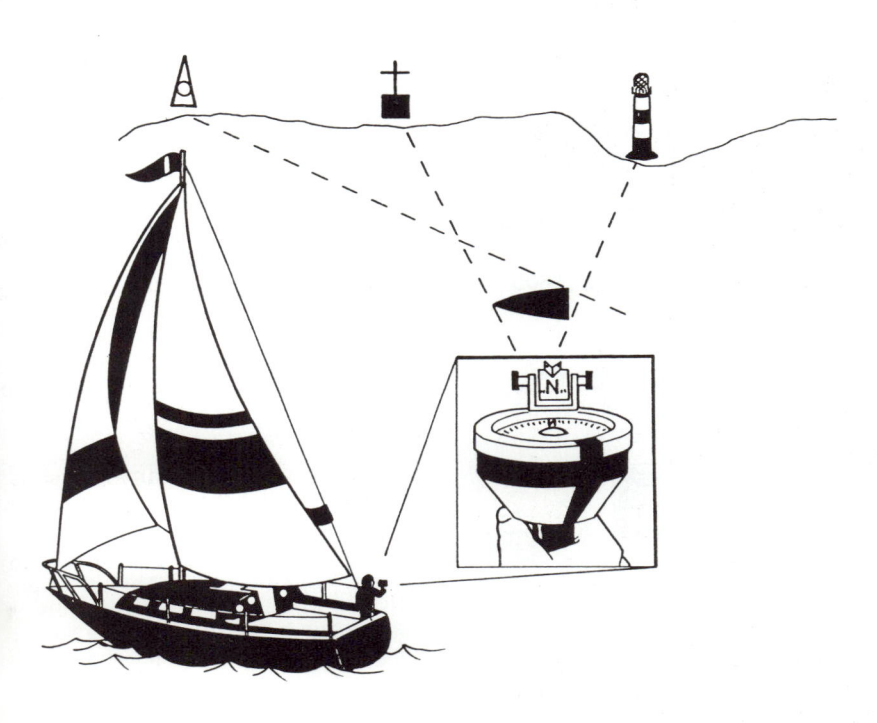

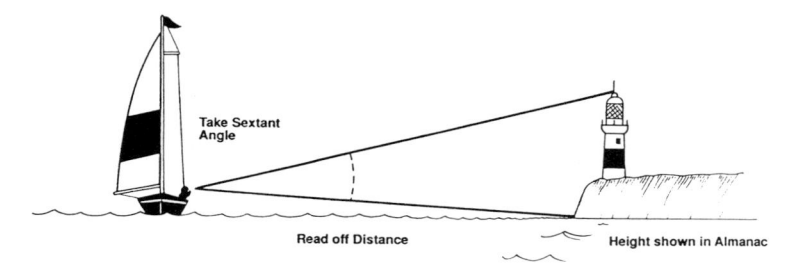

Vertical sextant angle

Using tables in Reeds Nautical Almanac, this will give you a distance off high objects.

Estimated position

When you cannot see to fix your position by the above method, you can estimate your position. This is complicated but interesting. You need to know the distance the vessel has travelled since the last known position and the course taken. To these factors must be added details of tides, currents and winds which will have affected the vessel's position.

For example, from a given position A at 0530 you follow a course of 165 degrees for an hour and cover a distance of 6 nautical miles. Information given on the chart about tides tells you that a tide of 3.8 knots was running in the direction of 102 degrees at 0600 in the area.

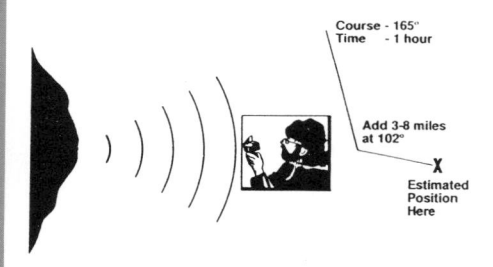

Plot the course of 165 degrees and a distance of 6 miles, then add a distance of 3.8 miles (3.8 knots for one hour) at 102 degrees. This gives you your approximate position, but as soon as possible, verify it by reference to visual objects.

Remember

All markings on a chart must be done with a soft pencil, preferably 2B.

There is some information on chart work in the Master Seaman section.

- **Complete a navigation exercise by day on water and know how to find North by sun or stars.**

The navigation exercise is a chance to put into practice the skills of position finding and course setting which you have acquired. Much of what is loosely meant by *navigation* is strictly pilotage; finding your way around by using buoys, bearings, transits, general observations, etc. Remembering that all of these are only aids to navigation, you must remember the three Ls: *lead* (how deep is the water), *log* (how far have you come) and *lookout*.

In a tideway where such an exercise is most likely to be held whether in canoe, yacht, sailing dinghy or whatever, the use of a single bearing and transits is often likely to be a great help. In particular if you are going across the tide you can allow for set, if you are going against it you can see that you really are (or are not) actually making progress relative to the land.

The view of a nearby tree and distant house at one time and a few minutes later indicate movement to the right.

North is found from the sun, by pointing the small hour hand of an analogue watch to the sun. However, the watch must strictly be set to Greenwich Mean Time (one hour earlier than B.S.T.). South is halfway between the hand and the twelve; North is right opposite of course. In practice even a cursory glance at the sun and an awareness of the time of day gives some idea of direction.

North by the stars is not so easy. You need to recognise **Polaris** or the North Star which is rather brighter than the others around it, and being well clear of the plane of the planets, should not be mistaken for a planet. However, you cannot even then be sure without checking how it fits with at least one of several other star formations. Only practice helps you identify them, but this sketch may help you. Note, though, that the whole sky appears to rotate, and therefore these formations may be the other way up! The task is not made any easier by a few thousand other fairly conspicuous stars, or the bright moon dazzling one, or even light cloud cover. But the technique is often useful on land and on the water, and later star recognition may help you with astro-navigation.

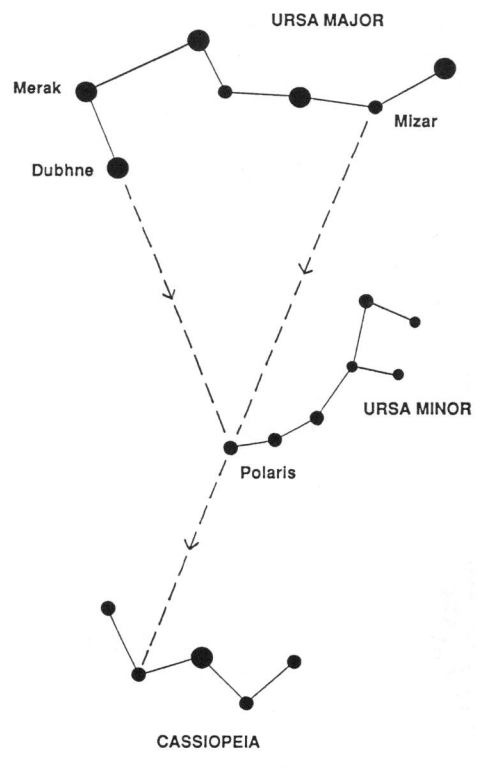

Navigation

- **Demonstrate how to take soundings in local water, both with leadline and pole.**

In practice you will often want to know how deep the water is when you have no sophisticated equipment (e.g. echo sounder, charts, etc) to help you. You may be navigating in a creek, or wanting to know if it is deep enough to roll a canoe, or wanting to know how much anchor cable to let out, or wanting to know if it is deep enough to moor your launch or whatever.

Often the simplest thing is to stick down an oar, paddle or some other pole and that will give you the answer. If it is deeper and you are stationary you can lower a weight attached to a line, and feel when it reaches the bottom. If you are moving then this lead needs to be thrown ahead of the vessel and hauled in (you will be surprised how quickly!) to feel the depth when it is up and down.

If you are anchoring a small vessel, you will probably want to let out anchor cable at least three times the depth of water as explained earlier. Then you can simply count the number of handfuls of cable required to reach the bottom, and then let out twice as much again, and usually a little bit more to be safe.

Ropework and Tradition

- **Hoist the colours for a Sea Scout Group. Make the 'Still' and 'Carry On' on a Bosun's Call.**

Sea Scouts use the Red Ensign, and in the case of the hundred Royal Navy Recognised Groups this is defaced with the Scout Badge and the Admiralty Crown.

No rigid ceremonial procedure is prescribed for Sea Scouts, but the following is typical:

The Troop is called to the alert, and turned towards the colours. 'Duty P.L.' is called, and he/she moves smartly to the foot of the ensign staff. The *still* is sounded (see opposite), and all salute while the duty P.L. hoists the ensign with dignity to the gaff. The P.L. steps back and salutes, the *carry on* is sounded, the salute ends, and the P.L. returns to his/her Patrol.

There should be a blue Scout pennant at the masthead.

BOSUN'S CALL

The Bosun's Call is a very old means of passing on orders and was often better than the human voice, since the sound was unlikely to be confused.

The instrument is called the 'Call'; the various patterns of sounds made on it are called 'Pipes'.

Hold the call between the first finger and the thumb of the right hand with the thumb on the shackle and the side of the buoy resting against the palm. The note is produced by blowing down the gun, the pitch being altered by reducing or increasing the amount of air blown in and by raising and lowering the fingers over the hole. Make sure that you do not touch the sides of the hole at the end of the gun or in the buoy as this will choke the note.

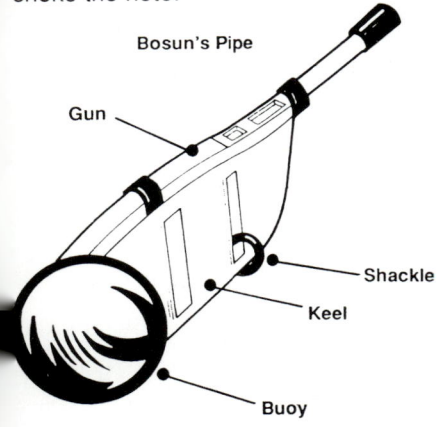

Bosun's Pipe
Gun
Shackle
Keel
Buoy

To make the two pipes 'Still' and 'Carry On' you will have to make two notes. The higher one is more difficult, since your finger is placed over the hole and stops the air getting out. The lower note is made simply by blowing through the unobstructed call.

The Still

This brings all hands to attention as a sign of respect, or to order silence or to stop working. It is made by holding the fingers over the buoy, the note being held for eight seconds.

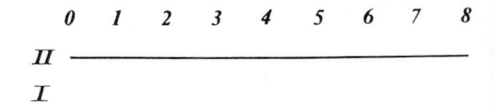

$$0 \quad 1 \quad 2 \quad 3 \quad 4 \quad 5 \quad 6 \quad 7 \quad 8$$

II ─────────────────
I

The Carry On

This is an order which means what it says. Start with the throttled note and change it at once to the lower. Hold for another second and stop sharply.

I   'Open' or 'Normal' note.
II 'Higher' or 'Throttled' note.

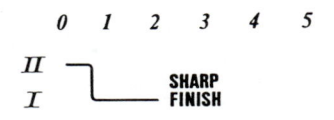

$$0 \quad 1 \quad 2 \quad 3 \quad 4 \quad 5$$

II ⎤
I   ⎦──── **SHARP FINISH**

- **Demonstrate three further calls commonly used in a Sea Scout Group.**

In spite of the simplicity of the Bosun's Call, a great variety of sounds can be made, and you may enjoy using these two techniques.

Wavering the breath, blowing alternately lightly and rather harder produces an attention catching warble.

The use of the tongue against the roof of the mouth as when you roll an R makes a shrill sound, as in a pea whistle.

Ropework and Tradition

Now try combining sounds with the pitch control to see if you can make these calls:

'General' or 'Away boat's crew' (often precedes announcements).

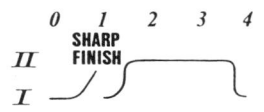

```
    0  1   2   3   4
       SHARP
   II  FINISH
   I
```

'Haul away'. (Also used to greet dignitaries.)

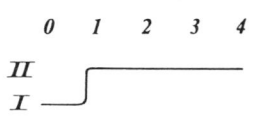

```
    0  1   2   3   4
   II
   I
```

- **Make a sailmaker's whipping and one other type of whipping.**

Even if the ends are melted, ropes are still likely to fray and so whipping should be used. For a stranded rope the Sailmaker's whipping is quickly done and yet very secure. Each strand of the rope should be sealed. The diagram illustrates how this is done. Experience has shown that the total length of the whipping should be about one third to half the thickness of the rope only, though many texts illustrate much longer whippings.

A simple but effective whipping is West Country whipping, which can also be used on braided ropes. Firstly, middle the whipping twine, tie it tightly round the rope with a thumb knot, and then work towards the end of the rope with a series of thumb knots every half turn as illustrated. Finish with a reef knot.

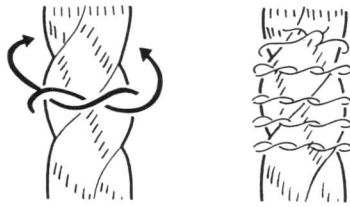

Those keen on ropework may wish to investigate the common whipping and American whipping - both quickly done but not very lasting - and the palm and needle whipping which is not often used as it takes a long time but is clearly the best.

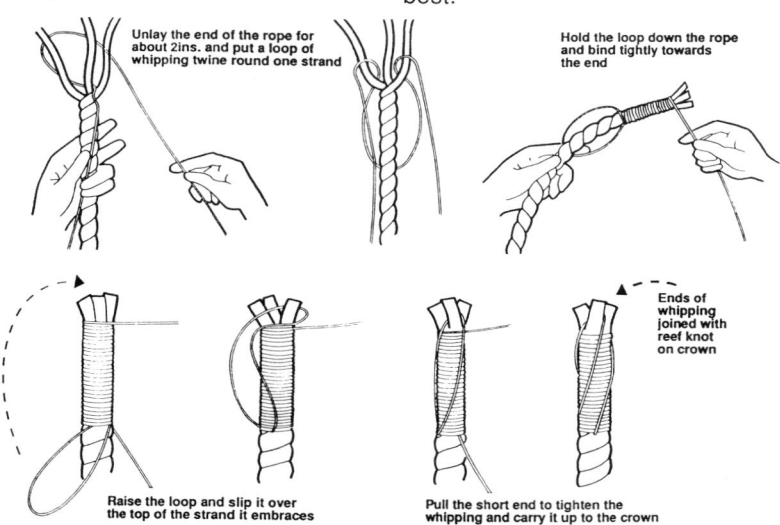

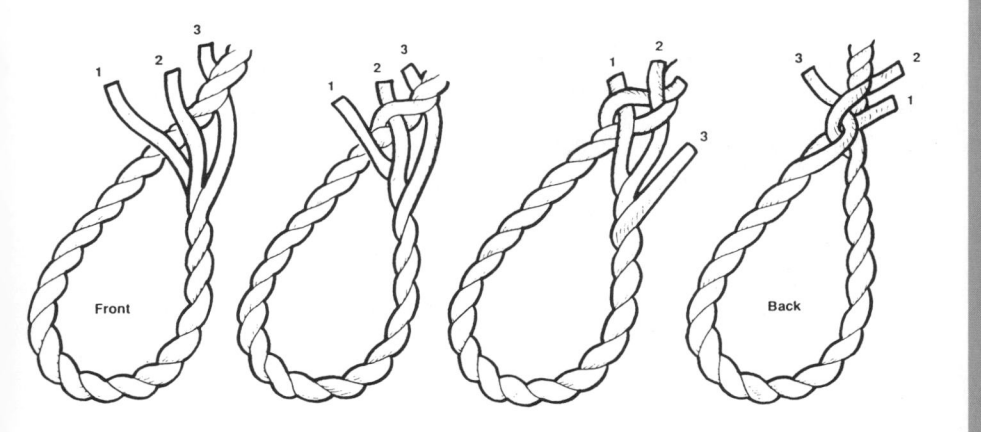

Eye Splice

The eye splice makes a very useful permanent eye in the end of a rope. The back splice deals with the ends so they do not fray, and can be done quickly when you are practised. However, it does make the end of the rope fatter which is no good if the rope has to be rove through blocks, etc. Further information is given in *Scout Pioneering* by John Sweet.

Back Splice

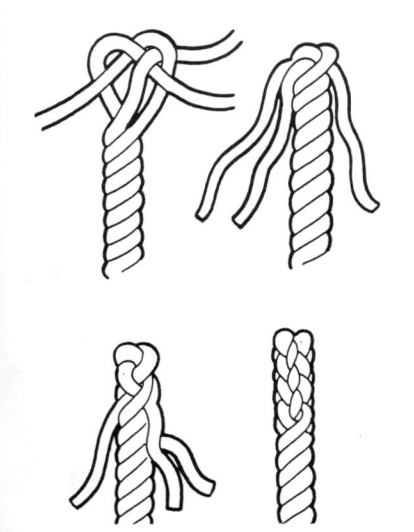

Short Splice

This is a very good way of permanently bending two stranded ropes together. The same comments as for the other splices apply.

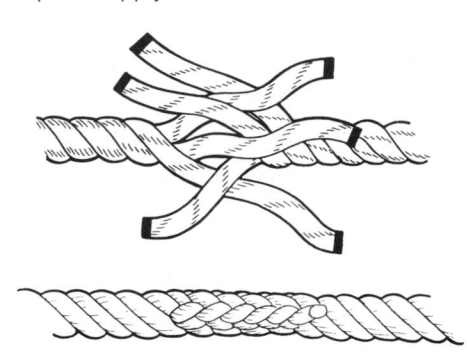

Ropework and Tradition

- **Demonstrate in a nautical setting the following and their correct uses: clove hitch, rolling hitch, fisherman's bend and a form of stopper knot.**

More information is given in *Scout Pioneering* for tying these. The uses given are typical but there are plenty more!

Clove Hitch

Temporary mooring; securing fenders; stopping a coil. May not stand flapping or jerking. Very quick and easy to do, including in the middle of a rope.

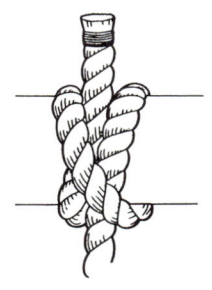

Rolling Hitch

Stronger than a clove hitch, and withstands sideways pull. Under the right conditions it will stand enormous sideways pull in a way that no other knot will. Can be used for securing a line (for example, a flag halyard) to a shroud, for use as a stopper (taking the weight off a cleat, for example),and guys on an awning (or tent).

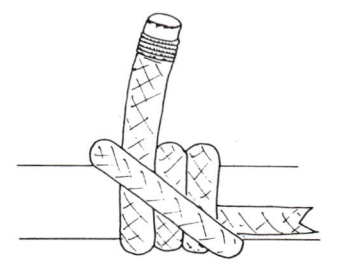

Fisherman's Bend

Enormously strong but can jam. Used in situations where something more permanent than a round turn and two half hitches is wanted, e.g. securing cable to the anchor, lanyard to a bucket.

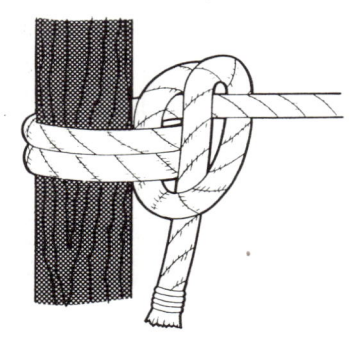

Stopper Knot

There are many types of stopper knot. The figure of eight knot is just one. It is used to make a lump in the end of a rope so that it will not run through the block. It is also suitable for 'first aid' treatment to stop a rope fraying. It will not jam.

- **Make a rope fender or a decorative piece of ropework, e.g. a lanyard.**

Rope Fender

A fender suitable for a pulling boat is made by doubling back a piece of stout rope and putting on a seizing to form an eye (A), with another at the length of which the fender is to be (B) and a good length of free ends for working back over it. Unlay the strands. Work them back over the parallel parts in a series of crown knots (C). Wall knots could be used (tucking ends upwards instead of downwards as in the crown knot), or use each alternatively. A series of crown knots makes the thickest fender. When the eye is reached, seize the ends below it and cut off any surplus (D).

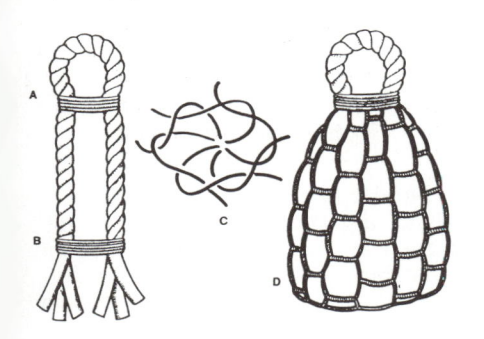

Lanyard

A lanyard or other decorative line can be made of a series of plaits or sennits. Simplest is the three-strand (E), but any number can be used providing it is remembered that parts must cross alternately up and down (F), over and under. For a flexible plait, suitable for the part of a lanyard around the neck, a ariat plait can be used with four strands as in some telephone cables) (G).

Work with opposite pairs of strands. Cross one pair (H), then cross the other pair (J). The crossings must be the same way to get the plait into its correct form. For the main decorative part of a lanyard the Portuguese sennit or boatswain's plait is suitable. This can be finished flat (K) or twisted (L). The work is done with cord or, in this case, two parts of the same cord (M); the outer parts being much longer than the core parts to allow for the amount used up in plaiting.

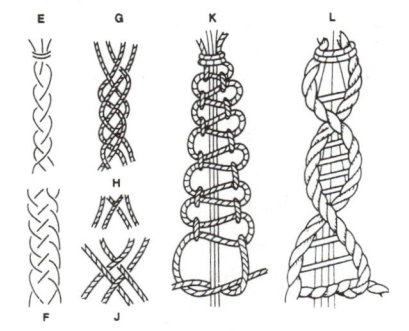

This is done by making a series of overhead knots. Stretch the core (N) and pass one working end behind (P), then the other under it, across and down through its loop (Q). Pull the ends crosswise to tighten. Do the same below it, the opposite way (R). Continue doing this on alternate sides and the result will be a flat plait (K). To make a twisted plait, make the first move each time from the same side and the plait will automatically take up a twisted form (L).

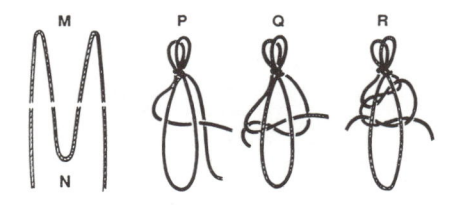

Ropework and Tradition

- **Demonstrate the correct method of maintaining and stowing ropes. Explain the differences in usage and stowage of natural and synthetic ropes.**

All ropes are best stowed dry, with any salt having been washed off first, and this is essential with natural fibre ropes. In practice this means that, where possible, the stowage wants to be in the open where ropes will hang freely and dry.

Protect ropes from chafing, chemicals, heat, kinks, sharp bends, etc. If they wear constantly in the same place, it may be possible to protect them with polythene tubing at that spot, or by changing them end for end.

Good coiling is important if you want the ropes to be ready for quick action, as it is infuriating when they are not, and might even be dangerous. Stranded ropes must be coiled clockwise, particularly if they are long, otherwise no end of kinks will appear when they are undone. (Very rarely you might come across a left handed rope, as on the World Scout Badge, which needs coiling anti-clockwise.)

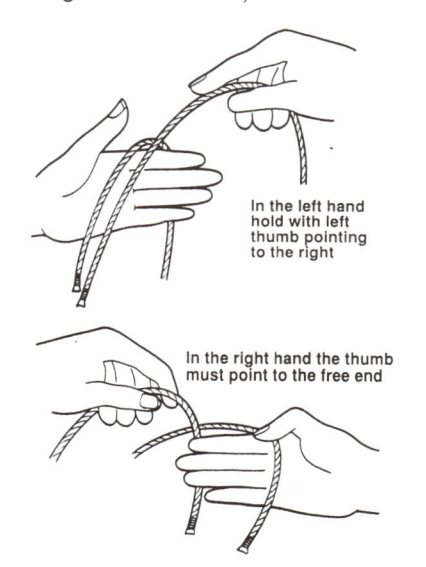

In the left hand hold with left thumb pointing to the right

In the right hand the thumb must point to the free end

Braided ropes can be coiled either way, but they do seem to prefer always being coiled the same way, therefore if you get in the habit of coiling these clockwise, too, it might help.

Often you will need to coil a rope which has a fixed end, for instance a halyard. In these cases it is important that you start coiling from the fixed end so that the turns can come out of the rope as you coil it.

The coils in the rope need to be a suitable size to make it manageable; experience will make it obvious approximately what size suits each length and size of rope. A typical line about 20 metres in length will need coils the size of almost a full arm stretch, whilst very long ropes will need coiling on the ground as the coils will have to be much too large to hold.

For normal coiling hold the rope as illustrated and apply a slight twist to each turn as you put it on to make the coil lie flat.

Types of Rope to Use

Invariably synthetic ropes are used afloat, largely because they do not rot. Here is an idea of what rope to use for what, but you'll have to compromise against cost, and you'll have to decide what diameter you need.

Halyards:

Pre-stretched Terylene, braided or stranded.

Sheets:

Normal Terylene. Braided is much easier on the hands.

Mooring:

Polypropylene is a common choice; it floats and is cheaper. Expensive nylon is strong and elastic; some pay extra for this.

Anchors:

In small craft Terylene is usual, but again nylon or an expensive cable layed rope is better for large vessels.

When you have coiled the rope it needs stopping. The method shown keeps the coil in good shape even if it is handled a lot, although sometimes the rope is rather kinked when you undo it.

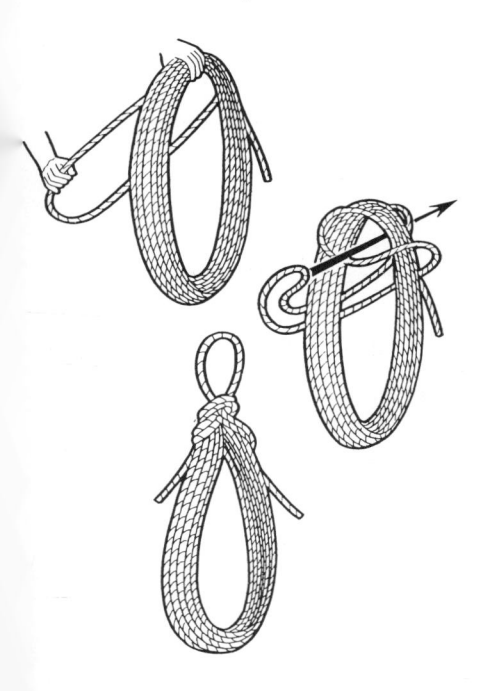

Meteorology

- **Know the Beaufort wind and sea scales.**

In 1805 Admiral Sir Francis Beaufort compiled wind and sea scales which have since been internationally accepted. These scales, which cover conditions from a gentle breeze to a hurricane, mean that yachtsmen will know very quickly what conditions they can expect; after all, to broadcast *'Cromarty: westerly gale force 8 imminent'* is a great deal quicker than having to say: 'The wind will be 33 to 40 knots, westerly, and the sea will be rough and disturbed with a lot of well marked foam streaks; the waves will be about 5 metres high between Duncansby Head and Aberdeen within the next six hours'.

The part of the scale we have produced here shows the readings from 0 - 8; in fact the readings go right up to force 17 when the wind speed is between 109 and 118 knots! The readings for forces 9 - 17 are described as severe gales, storms and hurricanes. You should not be out in them!

The requirement for this badge says that you must know the Beaufort Scale. To be able to do this well you will need to study the chart very carefully and have a fair knowledge of the characteristics of wind forces 0 to 8 - you are not expected to be word perfect but for your own safety you would be wise to make a real effort to master these points.

Meteorology

Beaufort Force	Speed in Knots	Descriptive Term	Effect on Open Sea	Effect on Shore	Effect on Dinghy
0	0	Calm	Glassy	Smoke rises vertically	Drifting
1	1-3	Light air	Scale like ripples	Smoke shows wind direction	May be difficult to make way over current – crew sits on lee side
2	4-6	Light breeze	Small wavelets with glassy crests	Leaves rustle	Wind felt on face – sails fill – crew amidships
3	7-10	Gentle breeze	Large wavelets – crests begin to break	Leaves and twigs in constant motion	Helmsman and crew sit inboard on weather side
4	11-15	Moderate breeze	Small waves, few white horses	Paper blows around, washing on line blows out	Light dinghies may need sitting out
5	16-20	Fresh breeze	Moderate waves, many white horses	Small trees sway, washing on line flutters	Sit out most dinghies, ease sheets in gusts – may need to reef
6	21-26	Strong breeze	Large waves, white crests everywhere, some spray	Large branches move	One, possibly two reefs needed
7	27-32	Near gale	Sea heaps up, white foam blown into streaks from breakers	Whole trees in motion	Drop mainsail and bring dinghy home under jib
8	33-40	Gale	Sea rough and disturbed, well marked streaks of foam	Branches snapped off, small trees blown down, difficulty walking against it	You should not be out!

- **Identify the basic types of cloud. Explain how they are formed, how wind speed is measured and how weather can affect water activities.**

The following are the most common types of cloud:

  Stratus - layers; horizontal
  Nimbus - rainy; dark
  Cumulus - puffy; vertical
  Cirrus - high; ice crystals
  Fracto - broken
  Alto - medium height

The sketches show typical formations. However, these are much more clearly shown in photographic texts.

In a nutshell, clouds are formed by warm air absorbing water as it passes over the oceans. However, the amount of water air can hold gets less as the temperature drops, therefore, when this happens clouds or rain occur. An important cause of cooling air is adiabatic cooling - cooling due to expansion with loss of pressure as air rises. High land and fronts are obvious causes of rising air.

Meteorology

Stratus
Layers Horizontal Featureless Layer
20,000 to 40,000 feet

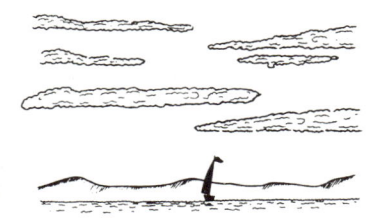

Cirrus – High Ice Crystals
20,000 to 40,000 feet

Nimbus – Rainy Dark Anvil Shape
Base to Top 10,000 to 60,000 feet

Fracto – Broken

Cumulus – Puffy Vertical
Base to Top 8,000 – 45,000 feet

Alto – Medium Height – Flat Base
8,000 to 20,000 feet

Meteorology

Wind speed is measured by anemometers in knots for nautical use. A knot is a nautical mile per hour, which is a little more than a statute mile per hour, the unit used on the land. (For the mathematical, a statute is 5280 feet, a nautical mile is 6076 feet.)

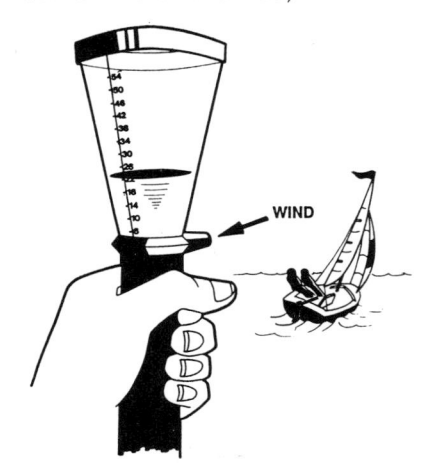

In open water strong winds increase danger, particularly if the wind comes against the tide, for it will get rougher and the demands on people and equipment may reach a limit very suddenly. The effect of wind is obvious in sailing craft, but do not forget that it affects all craft.

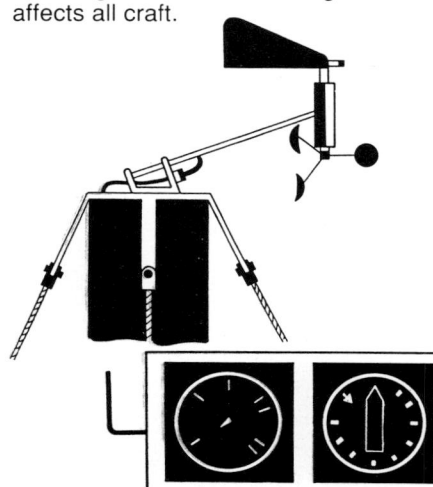

Large lakes become dangerous in strong winds, too. Usually there is not the same *fetch* as in open sea (distance to the land in the direction of the wind), but fresh water is whipped up more quickly as it is lighter, and often winds rush unexpectedly down mountainous slopes catching one unawares.

Small rivers are obviously less affected, but still can be much colder and thereby sap people's reserve of energy. Wind has a particularly powerful cooling effect when one is wet, seriously increasing the danger of hypothermia.

Sailing in open waters or large expanses of water does not only have the hazard of wind and associated roughness, but also bad visibility which is dangerous. Even with a compass, navigation can be hazardous, especially if there are other vessels using the same water (but even then if other vessels are using radar they may not be able to detect small craft) or strong tides.

Sunshine makes water activities appealing and tempts one out, often without suitable safety equipment or clothing for a possible change. But unexpected changes do occur; sudden wind, sea breezes, wind against tide, summer haze changing to fog and so on.

- **Identify the weather associated with frontal systems...**
- **Explain how temperature and pressure are measured...**
- **Identify the weather conditions associated with...**
- **Derive the geostrophic wind speed from...**
- **Be able to interpret a weather map...**

These are all covered in the factsheet on Meteorology available from the Resource Centre at Gilwell Park.

- **Record a shipping forecast, make a weather map from it, and be able to interpret it.**

Shipping forecasts give a great deal of information very systematically, and at speed but in mainly predictable form. To make full value of the forecast you need to interpret the information in a way that gives you a picture of the weather all around you, and likely to affect you within the next few days. This might be important, for instance, for deciding whether or not to take a small vessel across the English Channel, when you know you will also have to make the return journey a couple of days later.

One is always well advised to record the shipping forecast on tape before trying to write it down; then you can listen again if necessary. You will need to write it down to make the required weather map. Record the forecast using one of the pro-forma which are marketed - an extract is given below. The information will be given in the order made out on the form.

Meteorology

Scouts

GENERAL SYNOPSIS		at	............GMT/BST................		
System	Present position	Movement	Forecast position		at

Gales	SEA AREA FORECAST	Wind (At first)	Wind (Later)	Weather	Visibility
	VIKING				
	N. UTSHIRE				
	S. UTSHIRE				
	FORTIES				
	CROMARTY				
	FORTH				
	TYNE				
	DOGGER				
	FISHER				
	GERMAN BIGHT				
	HUMBER				
	THAMES				
	DOVER				
	WIGHT				
	PORTLAND				
	PLYMOUTH				
	BISCAY				
	FINISTERRE				
	SOLE				
	LUNDY				
	FASTNET				
	IRISH SEA				
	SHANNON				
	ROCKALL				
	MALIN				
	HEBRIDES				
	MINCHES				
	BAILEY				
	FAIR ISLE				
	FAEROES				
	SE ICELAND				
	Mark gale areas	Connect areas grouped in forecast			

COASTAL REPORTS at .... BST/GMT	Wind Direction	Force	Weather	Visibility	Pressure	Change	COASTAL REPORTS	Wind Direction	Force	Weather	Visibility	Pressure	Change
Sumburgh							Channel Light Vessel						
Fife Ness							Scilly						
Bridlington							Ronaldsway						
Dover							Malin Head						
Royal Sovereign							Tiree						
Jersey							Butt of Lewis						

Meteorology

From the recorded forecast ... *low 998 100 miles south of Iceland moving north west, expected Faroe by 1600 Sunday. High 1015 Biscay, stationary.*

Thames, Dover, Wight variable 2-3 becoming south westerly 3; fair; moderate but locally poor.

Varne south east 1, fair 500 metres, 1012 rising slowly.

Tiree south west 5, rain in last hour, 8 miles, 992 falling rapidly.

The general synopsis and reports from coastal stations give you the clues for producing the weather map. Highs, lows, ridges, fronts, etc. can be marked on direct, and the wind direction is, of course, just a little inside the isobars of the weather map.

The sea around the United Kingdom is divided into areas which are given names for easy reference.

The sea area Trafalgar is South of Finisterre.

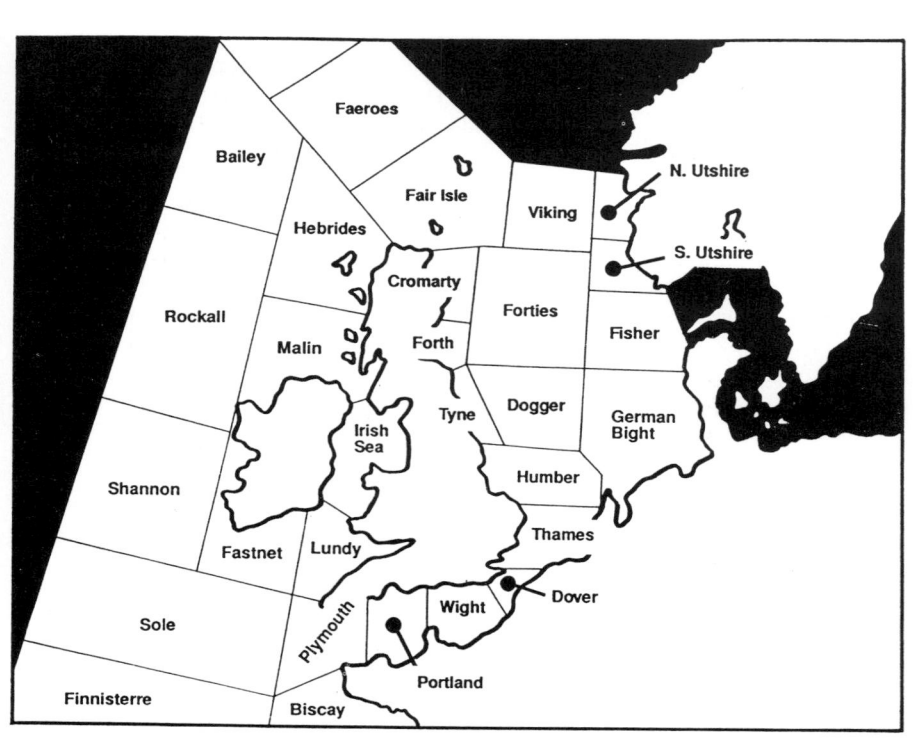

Rule of The Road and Communications

- **Know the rules for getting afloat on tidal waters and those of access to inland waters.**

1. There are rights of way on most tidal waters up to the high tide mark, though occasionally the low tide mark is the rule. However, various harbour authorities are entitled to charge.

2. The actual site where you can launch a vessel may be private, or there may be a charge for using the access. Main slipways usually have a notice telling you about launching there.

3. Various publications tell you where you can launch. Other users can advise you, of course.

4. Many inland waterways charge river dues, for instance the National Rivers Authority, the Norfolk Broads, etc. The onus is on you, the user, to find out first. Other users are an obvious source of information.

5. The riparian (river bank access) rights on many good canoeing waters are guarded strictly by landowners, who charge others to fish. Access to many apparently good waters is, therefore, illegal. However, local BCU and Scout personnel may well be able to tell you how to get permission for access onto such waters.

6. Some yacht clubs, local education authorities and other bodies are given (or sold) the boating rights on some inland waters. You need their permission before using these waters.

Safety

- **Know the distress, storm, fog and danger signals.**

You will have to find out for yourself what rules apply in your local waters. Every stretch of water will have its own characteristics and local knowledge will have established rules for the safety of users. Get in touch with your local Water Activities Adviser.

Unfortunately, problems do occur and vessels need to send distress signals. You should be able to recognise them, so that you can get help. You also need to be able to send them in case the problem is your own!

To be in distress means to need help *urgently*. It is of the utmost importance to know how to attract attention and vital for everyone that distress signals are given properly and only when absolutely necessary.

The most useful to you are:

S

O

S

Communication, Safety and Rules

75

S.O.S.

The signal can be given in Morse using a torch or by sound.

● ● ● — — — ● ● ●

Arm signals

Slowly raise and lower your arms at your side. Hold something bright or make the action bigger by holding oars to be seen over bigger distances.

Noise

Make a continuous sound. In different vessels this may be done by any means from sounding a fog horn to firing a gun! Ringing a bell or blowing on a whistle is more likely to be practical for you.

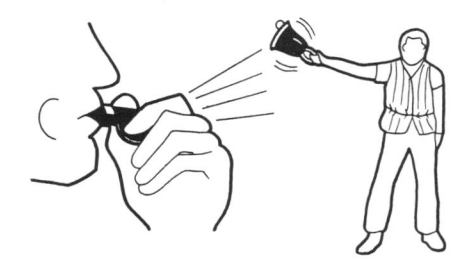

Orange smoke and red flares

These are recognised as distress signals.

Unusual objects

Hoisting an unusual object may attract attention.

Mayday

Means 'help!' (from the French 'M'aider').

Communication, Safety and Rules

International Code

The International Code distress signal is NC.

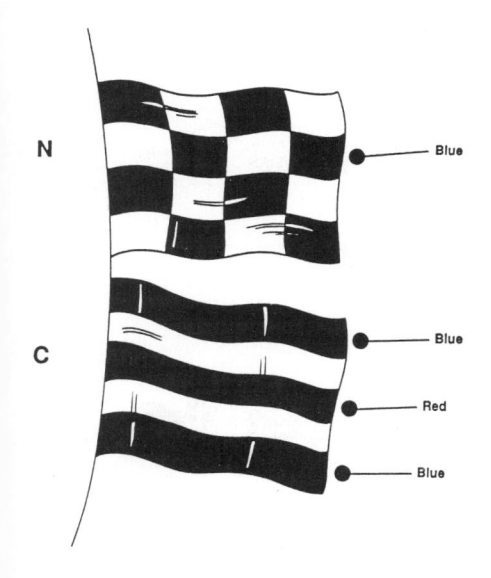

N — Blue

C — Blue, Red, Blue

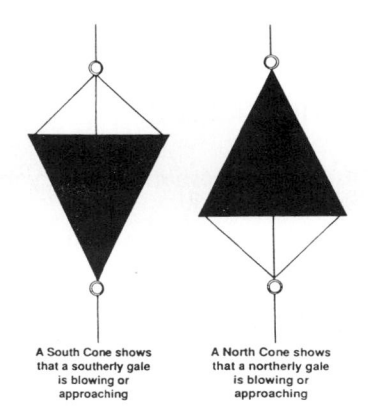

A South Cone shows that a southerly gale is blowing or approaching

A North Cone shows that a northerly gale is blowing or approaching

If a vessel is approaching danger without knowing it, another vessel, lighthouse or Coastguard Station may warn her by signalling continuously the Morse letter U, using a whistle, siren or lamp. Alternatively, the International Code of Signal flags for U or NF may be flown. If the ship does not take heed of the warning, further warning may be given by using a white flare, a rocket bursting with white stars or an explosive signal.

Where visibility is restricted, vessels have to make a noise to let others know where they are.

DANGER SIGNALS

Storm, fog and danger signals.

Danger signals are given when there is an immediate danger. Remember, you have to be able to recognise them as well as make them. There are also warnings about bad conditions and danger and these are also important.

While gale warnings are broadcast for the whole country, local conditions are reported by the Coastguard Station.

The hoisting of cones is one way of showing that storms are expected.

There are no East and West cones. So, North and South cones refer to all directions North or South of an East West line.

Fog Signals	
Signal	Means
Powered vessels One prolonged blast every two minutes	Powered vessel making way
Two prolonged blasts, with a two second interval in between, sounded every two minutes	Powered vessel temporarily stopped
All vessels One prolonged blast followed by two short blasts sounded every two minutes	Sailing vessel making way / vessel restricted in its ability to manoeuvre
Five second ringing of bell forward at one minute intervals	Any vessel under 100m at anchor
Five second ringing of bell forward followed by another five second sound of gong from the after part of the vessel at intervals of not more than one minute	Vessel more than 100m at anchor

Communication, Safety and Rules

77

THE BUOYAGE SYSTEM

- **Know the International Buoyage System (IALA).**

Here are two international systems of buoyage, the Lateral and the Cardinal, both of which are used in the British Isles. The Lateral system is based on two shapes of buoys; those with flat tops, can buoys, and those with pointed tops, conical buoys and they are used by the navigator with relation to the floodtide. The system can be summed up in a phrase: cans to port and cones to starboard when going in the same direction as the flood tidal stream.

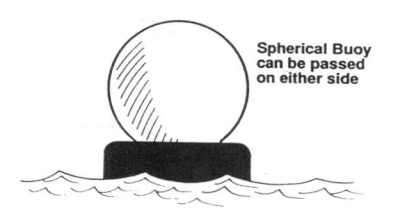

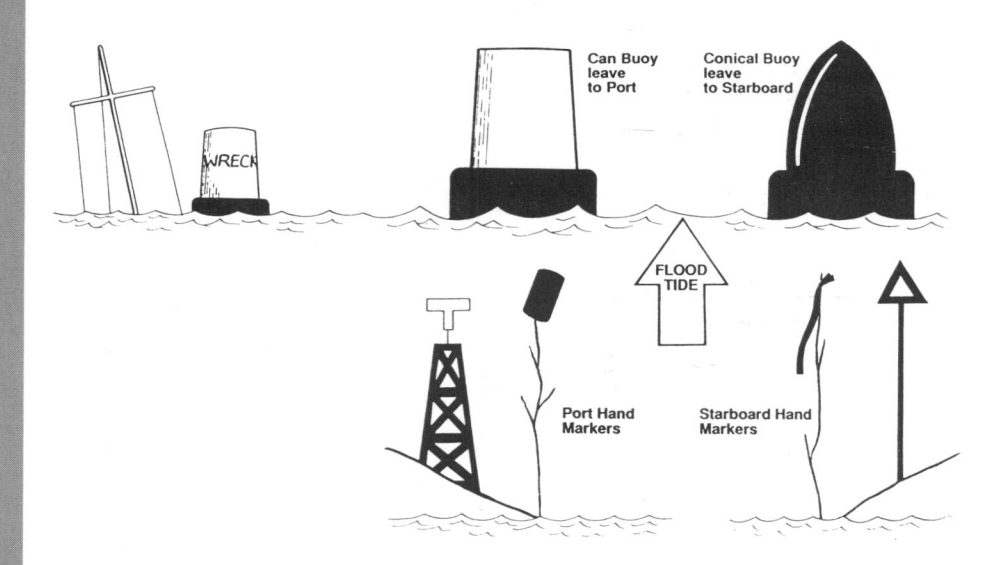

Spherical Buoy can be passed on either side

Can Buoy leave to Port

Conical Buoy leave to Starboard

WRECK

FLOOD TIDE

Port Hand Markers

Starboard Hand Markers

The cans are painted red, or red and white, and the conical ones are green. They come in all sizes from huge ones in a main shipping channel to marks in a creek, but the principle is the same, flat top or pointed. There are also spherical buoys. These are not very common and they can be passed on either side. There are other buoys for wrecks, sewer outflows, etc., which are other colours. The shapes, can or cone tell you which side you must leave them.

The cardinal system is simpler and it is used with relation to the cardinal points of the compass and is based on four different top-marks which are almost self-explanatory. All four top marks are combinations of two triangles. Both triangles pointing up tell you to keep to the North; both pointing down tell you to keep to the South; points together like an hour-glass, means 'keep to the West'. The final one, with the bases together, means 'keep to the East'.

SOUND SIGNALS

- **Know the sound signals used by powered vessels, under way or at anchor.**

Vessels give sound signals to indicate intended action when they can be seen.

One blast on a whistle or siren means: I am altering course to starboard.

Two blasts mean: I am altering my course to port.

Three blasts mean: My engines are going astern.

These signals are only given if there is a need to inform other vessels in order to avoid a collision.

If visibility is poor, the vessel needs to identify herself in some way and to indicate what she is doing. The following pattern of signals is recognised internationally.

Signal	made on	interval	means
One blast	whistle	for five seconds every 2 minutes	Power driven vessel making way
Two blasts	whistle	with interval of 2 seconds every 2 minutes	Power driven vessel stopped but not at anchor
One long and three short blasts	whistle	every 2 minutes	Given by vessel under tow
One long and two short blasts	whistle	every 2 minutes	I am manoeuvring with difficulty / I am towing / sailing vessel under way
Five seconds ringing	bell	every minute	Vessel at anchor
Three rings then five seconds rapid ringing then three rings	bell	every minute	Vessel aground

Communication, Safety and Rules

79

The following signals are normally made by a signalling lamp or with flags, but can also be given using a whistle. It is important that only one of these signals be given at a time, since they can easily be confused if blasts on the whistle run into each other. When giving Morse signals from a vessel, a dot lasts for one second, and a dash for five.

Morse	Letter	Meaning
● ● — ●	F	I am disabled; communicate with me
— — ●	G	I require a pilot
— ● —	K	I wish to communicate
● — ● ●	L	You should stop your vessel immediately
— — —	O	Man overboard
● — — ●	P	Your lights are out or burning badly
● ● ●	S	My engines are going astern
● ● —	U	You are standing into danger
● ● ● —	V	I require assistance
● — —	W	I require medical assistance

NAVIGATION LIGHTS

- **Know the navigation lights carried by different types of vessel. Identify at least three different types from the lights displayed.**

There are many combinations of navigation lights used by vessels at night. Basically, lights show you that the vessel is there and warn you to keep clear. It is hardly likely that you will come across all the possible combinations but here are some of the more common ones.

Rowing and small sailing boats need to carry no lights, but there should be a small lantern or a strong torch for use as necessary.

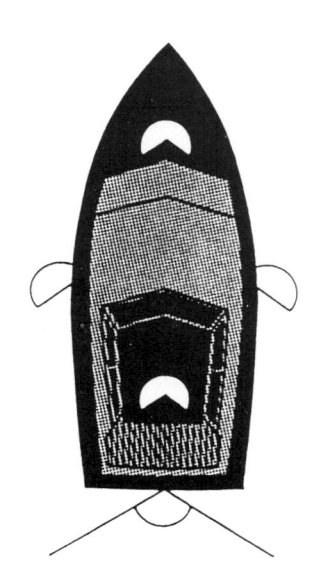

A power driven vessel of less than 50m in length, underway carries:

- 1 white steaming light
- port and starboard lights
- 1 stern or overtaking light

If the vessel is more than 50m in length, it carries an additional steaming light.

A vessel less than 50m in length at anchor carries:

- 1 white light where it can best be seen, visible all round.

If the vessel is more than 150m in length, it carries an additional light in the stern, visible all round.

The day signal for a vessel at anchor is a black ball hoisted in the fore part of the vessel.

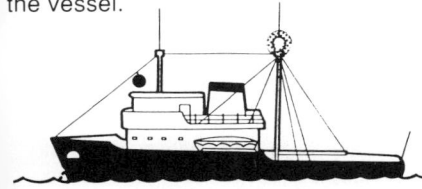

A power driven vessel towing another vessel, with a tow less than 200m (the tow is the distance from the stern of the vessel being towed).

Towing vessel carries:

- 2 steaming lights
- port and starboard lights
- 1 stern light
- 1 yellow towing light above the stern.

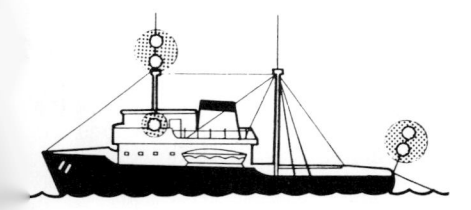

The towed vessel carries:

- port and starboard lights
- 1 stern light.

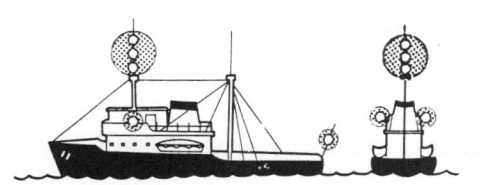

If the tow is more than 200m, a third steaming light is carried by the towing vessel.

A sailing vessel under way carries:

- port and starboard lights
- 1 stern light.

In addition she may carry a red light over a green light at the masthead.

Cable laying vessels and those engaged on surveying, underwater operations and picking up cable carry:

- a red over a white over a red light
- port and starboard lights
- 1 stern light.

If you see these lights when you are out at night, keep clear!

Communication, Safety and Rules

RACING RULES

- **Have a working knowledge of the International Yacht Racing Rules, and Portsmouth Yardstick Handicapping System.**

The full yacht racing rules are lengthy and complicated. These notes are certainly not intended to replace reference to the full rules or other explanations of them which have been published for the serious race helmsman. However, they should be helpful for the relative novice.

1. Sailing instructions published before the event will outline local rules, start procedures, briefing, etc.

2. No cheating! Methods of propulsion other than wind, using a vessel out of the class, deliberately breaking other rules are not to be contemplated.

3. Even if it is your right of way but a collision occurs, then you will be disqualified unless you tried to avoid the collision.

4. If you know you have broken a rule then you must retire promptly (unless the sailing instructions allow, for instance, a 720 degree turn).

5. The signals for starts are normally the raising and lowering of flags, carefully timed, with a sound signal to draw your attention to them.

   10 minute warning

   5 minute warning

   start

   class flag hoisted

   blue peter hoisted

   flags lowered

   If you are over the line at the start you must keep out of everyone else's way until you have recrossed the line. A sound signal will indicate that at least somebody was over the line at the start.

6. In open water, clear of marks and obstructions:

   Port tack yachts must give way to the starboard tack yachts. Both on same tack, the windward boat keeps clear. Overtaking vessel to windward keeps clear. Tacking or gybing - keep clear of others.

7. At obstructions:

   Hail any boats in your way if you must alter course; he **must** give you water.

8. At the mark of the course:

   Inside boat has right of way if he has overlap on the boats outside provided that it is established that the overlap occurred before two boat lengths from the buoy.

9. If you meet vessels which are not racing the normal rights of way prevail, though often they will try to keep out of your way.

Portsmouth Yardstick

Sailing races are obviously better if all the boats are identical, but in practice there are many occasions when boats of different classes race together.

A good attempt can be made to make the event fair by using the P.Y. Scheme. With this, all popular classes are given a number which relates to their average racing performance. The P.Y. numbers are updated each year by the RYA on the basis of further experience, and a new list published.

All vessels are timed to the nearest second as they race. Then the easiest way to apply the handicap is to use a calculator. Convert the race time into seconds, divide by the handicap, multiply by 100, and there you have the corrected time from which positions can be calculated.

You must recognise that the handicaps published are based on average performance, that is the next best that can be done. Clearly different weather conditions will still favour certain classes.

- **Know the effects of currents on non-tidal waterways and the effect of heavy rain up river, danger levels, rapids and wild waters on two rivers.**

- **Be able to advise on suitable mooring and anchorages locally for different types of craft, and emergency landing places for small craft.**

These two options both refer to your own local or regularly used waters. You will have to find the answers locally.

- **Explain the system of sea lanes in National and International waters.**

In the main busy shipping waterways there are lanes in which ships should proceed in a particular direction. This is just as with cars on the road, except that the boundaries are not marked, and you keep to the lane which is starboard. Where this applies it is clearly marked on up to date charts.

There are obligations on vessels crossing these lanes. Firstly, one must do so as near as practicable on a course at right angles to the main lanes. Secondly, vessels crossing must not impede the passage of those in the lanes. Taking a yacht across the lanes is sometimes compared with pushing a pram across a motorway. In light airs one is very likely to have to motor, however capable a sailor one is. If visibility is less than a couple of miles then it is even more important to keep up a good speed. In fog it is really not safe to proceed without radar, for you must be able to keep out of the way of the ships.

- **Obtain a Radio Yacht Licence**

V.H.F. radio is used in more and more vessels, and also by many yacht clubs, marinas, etc., so the possession of a licence is clearly a good thing. This enables one to install a radio, or to use someone else's without supervision.

The examinations are administered by the Royal Yachting Association, from whom full details are available.

Expeditions

Expeditions provide a splendid way both to demonstrate what you have learnt and to put it all into practice.

Steering by compass

This means by compass mounted in the boat. The mariner's compass is different from the land compass in that the compass card is the moving part.

In setting the compass course your leaders will have made allowances for wind, current and magnetic variation. Deviation in a pulling boat, will be so slight as to be negligible. Compass courses and bearings are usually signalled in true. Allow for compass error.

Taking charge

Being in charge is a big responsibility. You have to learn how to handle your crew and how to hand out jobs to them. Do not try to do too much yourself.

If you are in a day boat, the question of gear will be fairly simple. There is no reason why a decked craft should not be used, but the gear required will then be a more complex matter.

Checklist for day boats:
Safety equipment:
    oars/paddle on lanyard
    flares
    bailer/bucket on lanyard
    personal buoyancy
    proper clothing
    tools
    lights
    boat's bag
    anchor and cable.

Conditions of boat and fittings:
    bungs, gudgeon and pintle
    shackle pins, clevis pins
    running and standing rigging.

Rules:
    report procedure for safety check
    Boat inspection
    Water Authorisation
    Swimming.

If using a decked craft, remember to check everything. Never assume that anything works properly. You are the responsible person and you are doing your job properly if you know that everything is working properly and that the safety of all crew members has been as carefully catered for as possible.

PLAN YOUR OWN EXPEDITION... AND THE FUTURE

If you began your Scout training in the Beaver Scout Colony continuing through the Pack and into the Troop, intending still to go into the Venture Scout Unit, you will already know that expeditions, camping and visits play an important part in enjoying yourself and showing you to be responsible for yourself and for others.

Similarly, your progress through the stages of the badges will have shown you how to handle any kind of craft, how to work effectively with other people and how to get the best out of boating.

As you have grown up through the Movement, you will have had more and more opportunities of deciding on and planning your own activities and by the time you become a Venture Scout you will no longer be waiting for other people to do things for you. You will be capable of doing things yourself and will get much more satisfaction from working with other people on projects that you have thought up together, planned well and carried out effectively.

There are a number of Scout Association publications which deal very thoroughly with expeditions of all kinds and you should read these books to get an overall picture of what is involved in planning journeys and reaching objectives.

When you have been through the entire programme of training and covered all aspects of water activities dealt with in the requirements of the four badges, you will be qualified as someone who can be relied on to have, and be able to use, knowledge and skills useful to other people. You can wear the Master Seaman badge on your Venture Scout uniform when you join the Unit and there are many ways of maintaining your interest in water activities as you continue through the training for the Venture Scout and Queen's Scout Awards.

Expeditions

Books

There are no end of publications about various aspects of boating, aimed at all levels of experience, and most of them good value. The following are listed because they relate directly to references in the text.

BCU Coaching Handbook
British Canoe Union – 0 900082 03 8

Canoeing - Skills and Techniques
Neil Shave, Crowood Press – 0 946284 36 9

Dinghy Sailing Handbook
Royal Yachting Association – G3

RYA Young Sailors Logbook
Royal Yachting Association – G11/93

RYA Dinghy Certificate and Sailing Logbook
Royal Yachting Association – G4/93

The RYA also publish booklets on aspects of Powerboating, VHF Radio, Weather Forecasts, Board Sailing, Offshore Sailing etc. (RYA, RYA House, Romsey Road, Eastleigh, Hampshire, SO5 4YA.)

Scout Boating

Scout Boating